SIOP® Works for Early Engli...

From the authors and developers ... Observational Protocol (SIOP®) Model comes *Using the SIOP® Model with Pre-K and Kindergarten English Learners*. The newest addition to the SIOP® Model Series presents early childhood teachers and administrators, intervention specialists, and coordinators with precise lesson plans and activities for meeting the needs of their young learners.

Don't miss these other SIOP® Model resources for the classroom!

Making Content Comprehensible for English Learners: The SIOP® Model, Third Edition (ISBN: 0-205-51886-9)

The SIOP® Model for Teaching English-Language Arts to English Learners (ISBN: 0-205-62760-9)

99 Ideas and Activities for Teaching English Learners with The SIOP® Model (ISBN: 0-205-52106-1)

Making Content Comprehensible for Elementary English Learners: The SIOP® Model (ISBN: 0-205-62756-0)

The SIOP® Model for Teaching Mathematics to English Learners (ISBN: 0-205-62758-7)

Implementing The SIOP® Model Through Effective Professional Development and Coaching (ISBN: 0-205-53333-7)

Making Content Comprehensible for Secondary English Learners: The SIOP® Model (ISBN: 0-205-62757-9)

The SIOP® Model for Teaching History-Social Studies to English Learners (ISBN: 0-205-62761-7)

The SIOP® Model for Administrators (ISBN: 0-205-52109-6)

Response to Intervention (RTI) and English Learners: Making It Happen (ISBN: 0-13-704890-4)

The SIOP® Model for Teaching Science to English Learners (ISBN: 0-205-62759-5)

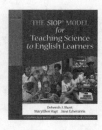

To learn about Pearson's SIOP® Training please visit **www.siopinstitute.net**

Using the SIOP® Model with Pre-K and Kindergarten English Learners

Jana Echevarría
California State University, Long Beach

Deborah J. Short
Center for Applied Linguistics, Washington, DC
Academic Language Research & Training, Arlington, VA

Carla Peterson
Iowa State University

Boston   Columbus   Indianapolis   New York   San Francisco   Upper Saddle River
Amsterdam   Cape Town   Dubai   London   Madrid   Milan   Munich   Paris   Montreal   Toronto
Delhi   Mexico City   Sao Paulo   Sydney   Hong Kong   Seoul   Singapore   Taipei   Tokyo

Vice President, Editor-in-Chief: *Aurora Martínez Ramos*
Editorial Assistant: *Meagan French*
Marketing Manager: *Danae April*
Production Editor: *Gregory Erb*
Electronic Composition and Editorial Production Service: *Nesbitt Graphics, Inc.*
Interior Design: *Nesbitt Graphics, Inc.*
Manufacturing Buyer: *Megan Cochran*
Photo Researcher: *Annie Pickert*
Cover Designer: *Linda Knowles*

For Professional Development resources visit www.allynbaconmerrill.com

Credits and acknowledgments borrowed from other sources and reproduced, with permission, in this textbook appear on the appropriate page within the text.

Photo Credits: pages 1, 10, 27, 45, 55, 65, 76: Annie Pickert/Pearson; pages 18, 96: Bob Daemmrich Photography

10 9 8 7 6 5   V031   15 14 13

www.pearsonhighered.com   ISBN-10: 0-13-708523-0
ISBN-13: 978-0-13-708523-1

Dedication

*To parents and ECE teachers—the front line educators
who introduce children to language and learning.*

Jana Echevarría is a Professor Emerita at California State University, Long Beach. She has taught in elementary, middle, and high schools in general education, special education, ESL, and bilingual programs. She has lived in Taiwan, Spain, and Mexico. An internationally known expert on second language learners, Dr. Echevarría is a Fulbright Specialist. Her research and publications focus on effective instruction for English learners, including those with learning disabilities. Currently, she is Co-Principal Investigator with the Center for Research on the Educational Achievement and Teaching of English Language Learners (CREATE) funded by the U.S. Department of Education, Institute of Education Sciences (IES). In 2005, Dr. Echevarría was selected as Outstanding Professor at CSULB.

Deborah J. Short is a professional development consultant and a senior research associate at the Center for Applied Linguistics in Washington, DC. She co-developed the SIOP® Model for sheltered instruction and has directed national research studies on English language learners funded by the Carnegie Corporation, the Rockefeller Foundation, and the U.S. Dept. of Education. She recently chaired an expert panel on adolescent ELL literacy. As the director of Academic Language Research & Training, Dr. Short provides professional development on sheltered instruction and academic literacy around the U.S. and abroad. She has numerous publications, including the SIOP® book series and five ESL textbook series for National Geographic/Hampton-Brown. She has taught English as a second/foreign language in New York, California, Virginia, and the Democratic Republic of Congo.

Carla Peterson is a professor in the Department of Human Development and Family Studies and the Associate Dean for Research and Graduate Studies for the College of Human Sciences at Iowa State University. Dr. Peterson earned a PhD at the University of Minnesota. She has worked in early care and education for 35 years as a teacher, administrator, teacher trainer, and researcher. She has worked in child care, Head Start, and early childhood special education settings. Her research and teaching have focused on designing interventions to meet children's individual needs within inclusive settings.

contents

We have written this book especially for you, the early childhood educator who works with young children in their first and most important years of schooling. You may be a kindergarten teacher, a pre-K classroom teacher, a child development center teacher, a child care provider, or an administrator who has responsibilities for a program. As such, you have experienced the large and growing numbers of young children who enter preschool and kindergarten speaking languages other than English. This trend has generated a lot of interest in using the SIOP® Model (Sheltered Instruction Observation Protocol) in these early childhood (ECE) settings. We hope that this book will help you provide an optimal learning environment for all your students.

We use several terms throughout this book to refer to young English learners and the settings in which they receive care and education. These terms include *early childhood education (ECE), pre-K, preschool, kindergarten,* and *early care and education*—terms that are used in different contexts and regions throughout the United States. While we understand that early childhood spans birth to age 8, the focus of this book is on classrooms serving preschool-aged children and kindergarteners. Further, early care and education is provided for preschoolers in a variety of settings, but for ease of communication, we call these *pre-K or kindergarten classrooms*. The individuals who work in these settings take on the role of teacher (and paraprofessional), and so we will use that term.

This book is specifically designed to address the needs of young children in pre-K or kindergarten for whom English is the language used in school and another language is spoken in their homes. Since the pre-K years provide an opportunity for all children to develop competency in language, these young learners are developing proficiency in their home language at the same time they are learning English. Youngsters who are not proficient speakers of English—the language of instruction in most cases—require accommodations so that they can be successful in school. The SIOP® Model provides a framework to guide teachers' interactions with English learners so that these students can participate fully in all aspects of early schooling.

We know that high-quality early childhood programs contribute to positive outcomes for children, including improved school readiness, higher academic achievement, lower dropout rates, higher high school graduation rates, and higher rates of college attendance (NAEYC, 2009). It is imperative that we offer the most effective and developmentally appropriate instructional setting possible for young English learners; implementation of the features of the SIOP® Model can be an important tool for doing that.

As you read this book, we ask you to think about how the features of the SIOP® Model can improve your practice as you work with the children in your program or class. Please keep in mind that, although they are discussed individually, the SIOP® Model's features are interrelated and support one another.

Organization and Purpose of This Book

It is our goal to make this book a very teacher-friendly resource for you, and so we have included information in accessible formats. To illustrate the SIOP® Model in action, in Chapters 4 through 8, we provide a sample lesson plan from lessons that we have observed or from programs with which we are familiar. These plans may be adjusted to fit the developmental levels of the children you work with.

Chapter 1: The SIOP® Model and Young Learners

In this first chapter, we introduce the focus of the book: using the SIOP® Model to teach English learners in preschool and kindergarten. We provide an overview of the SIOP® Model, its research support, and its application to early childhood education programs. We conclude the chapter with a discussion of the importance of professional development.

Chapter 2: Getting to Know Young English Learners and Early Childhood Programs

We introduce these young English learners, the fastest growing group of students in our schools, and also discuss some of the trends in early childhood education today. We present some demographic data that provides the context for the need for this book. Also discussed are some of the issues faced by English learner children, their families, and the schools that are committed to educating them.

Chapter 3: Language Development in Young English Learners

This chapter focuses on language development, which is the foundation of literacy development and plays such a large role in schooling. These children are learning language in the early years, both their home language and English, so understanding the importance of language in all learning is critical. Here, we explain how language is learned, the importance of first language and English language development, the role of parents in language development, and ways to assist the learning of children with special needs.

Chapters 4–7: Using the SIOP® Model with Young Learners

In each of these chapters, we address two components of the SIOP® Model and discuss how each feature of the component might be implemented with young learners. We provide a lesson plan that reflects the features discussed in the chapter as well as specific teaching ideas and activities to use in your classroom.

Chapter 8: Implementing the SIOP® Model in Preschool and Kindergarten: Sample Programs

In this chapter, we highlight several programs that have been using the SIOP® Model successfully in preschool and kindergarten classes. They include:

- Columbus Junction, IA—A preschool program in Roundy Elementary School
- Central Falls, RI—Veterans Memorial Elementary School kindergarten program
- Washington, DC—AppleTree Institute for Education Innovation Partnership includes three charter preschools: AppleTree Early Learning Public Charter School, D.C. Prep Academy, and Early Childhood Academy

Each program description offers a different type of implementation and we hope that the information provided might be applicable to your own setting.

Chapter 9: Effective Use of the SIOP® Protocol in Supporting Teachers

This chapter provides guidance for using the SIOP® protocol in preschool and kindergarten settings. We make the point that while the SIOP® protocol has numeric values that allow an observer to rate lessons, in the case of teachers of young learners, written feedback should be provided on lessons. Ratings (except for research purposes) are not appropriate, given the short duration of lessons and the level of instruction for young learners.

Appendix A

In Appendix A, we provide a copy of the SIOP® Model Checklist, a form that may be used for lesson planning as well as professional development and coaching activities.

Appendix B

In this Appendix we present both a comprehensive version of the SIOP® protocol as well as an abbreviated version. Please be sure to read Chapter 9: Effective Use of the SIOP® Protocol in Supporting Teachers, in which we have included a brief discussion of the way the protocol is used effectively to observe lessons and provide feedback to teachers. The comprehensive version of the protocol offers more description of the levels of implementation for each feature and allows for written comments on each.

Appendix C

The SIOP® Model is a research-validated approach for teaching English learners. As such we provide a discussion of a number of empirical studies that have been conducted in classrooms using the SIOP® Model. There are currently additional studies under way too. The information presented in Appendix C provides evidence of the SIOP® Model's effectiveness to date.

Acknowledgments

As with any such endeavor, we could not have written this book without the assistance of dedicated colleagues. In particular, we would like to thank the teachers who opened their classrooms to us and provided important insights into the day-to-day teaching and learning that occurs with English learners in early childhood classrooms. They include Chanty Lim, Tina Easter, and Dr. Linda James Perry, Long Beach Head Start, CA; Mardell Nash and Melinda Vittetow, Los Alamitos Unified School District, CA; Charlotte Daniel, Pearson Education; Cathy Fox, Central Falls School Department, RI; Leah Gonzalez, AppleTree Institute, Washington DC; Tara Paul, Columbus Junction, IA. We'd also like to acknowledge our co-authors on Chapter 2: Gayle J. Luze, Molly Luchtel, and Emily Worthington, whose assistance was invaluable. Special thanks to Sydney Luckey for her contribution. In addition we also acknowledge and appreciate the suggestions offered by the reviewers of this book: Joseph E. Leaf, Norristown Area School District, PA; Karen Wong, Kohwles Education Center, WA; and Sanjuanita Ybarra-Hana, Barlow Elementary, NJ. Finally, we want to express our gratitude to our editor, Aurora Martínez, for her vision in anticipating the need to address the schooling of early learners.

chapter 1

The SIOP® Model and Young Learners

Alejandro is excited because his teacher, Mr. Adolfo, poured some cooking oil into bottles of water and let each student have a bottle to hold. Alejandro shakes the bottle and watches the water move. He likes the noise it makes. He shows his friend, Juan, how every time the water stops moving, the oil settles on top again. He tries to mix it up, but it keeps separating. The boys shake their bottles very hard, but the water and oil won't mix. Mr. Adolfo said that the oil makes the water dirty, and it is called water pollution. The word *pollution* is written on the board next to a picture of dirty water. Mr. Adolfo points to the word when he talks about dirty water. Yesterday the class watched a short video about oil that had spilled into the ocean. Then they sang a song about clean and dirty water. It was fun because after the song,

Mr. Adolfo put a little brown paint on each child's hands and then they rinsed their hands in a bucket. The water was cold! The children squealed with delight. They saw the dirty water in the bucket. Water pollution! Today Mr. Adolfo placed interesting materials about pollution in several of the learning centers so that during play time, the idea of water pollution was again reinforced for the children.

Next door in Miss Lawrence's class, the children are sitting on the rug together and Miss Lawrence is telling them about pollution. Resundo has a hard time understanding what she is saying. The teacher has been talking for a very long time. He tries to sit still, but he wants to move around and play with his friends. Miss Lawrence scolds Resundo and Alex because they begin to whisper to one another and giggle. Finally, the teacher tells the children they can get up. Resundo hopes that now it is time to play with trucks, but Miss Lawrence tells the children to sit at the tables. Miss Lawrence hands each child a paper with a picture of water. She then tells the children to color the picture to show that the water is polluted. He doesn't know what that means. He looks around and the other children also seem unsure of what to do. Miss Lawrence says a lot of words, including *pollution.* She seems to be getting annoyed because some children don't know what to do with the paper and others aren't coloring the way she wants.

Although these two pre-K classrooms are in the same building, you can see that the teaching styles differ significantly. In Mr. Adolfo's class, children are actively engaged, using interesting hands-on materials, talking about and singing about the concept of water pollution. Their experience with learning is positive and fun. In Miss Lawrence's class, she is telling children about water pollution, but the verbal description is lost on them. She expects the children to sit quietly and listen to her. Children feel anxious because while they want to please the teacher, either they don't understand what she wants them to do or they are unable to do it.

What Is the SIOP® Model?

In this chapter, we introduce you to the SIOP® Model and provide you with an overview of how the model works with young children. The SIOP® Model is an approach to teaching English learners that encourages the kind of instruction seen in Mr. Adolfo's class.

The Sheltered Instruction Observation Protocol (SIOP®) Model was developed through a U.S. Department of Education funded research project to define the components of effective sheltered instruction lessons and investigate its impact on student learning (Please see Appendix C in Echevarria, Vogt, & Short, 2010a to learn about the development of the SIOP® Model). Also referred to as content-based ESL, SDAIE (specially designed academic instruction in English), and structured English immersion (SEI), sheltered instruction:

- Is a means for making grade-level academic content (e.g., science, social studies, math, language arts) more accessible for English learners. Teachers modify instruction so that it is comprehensible for students.
- Includes the practice of highlighting key language features and incorporating strategies that increase interaction and practice using language.

FIGURE 1.1 *SIOP® Terminology*

SIOP® Model = the lesson planning and delivery system

SIOP® protocol = the instrument used to observe, rate, and provide feedback on lessons

The SIOP® Model research project began as a way to design and validate an observation protocol for assessing the effectiveness of sheltered instruction lessons. Until that time, there wasn't an agreed upon model of exactly what constituted an effective sheltered (SEI, content-based ESL, or SDAIE) lesson. The model evolved into a lesson planning and delivery system that guides teachers in implementing effective lessons. So, the SIOP® term applies to both the observation instrument for rating fidelity of lessons to the model and the instructional model for lesson planning and delivery (see The SIOP® Model Checklist, Appendix A). Figure 1.1 shows the terminology used to distinguish between these two uses. Details about how to use the SIOP® protocol are found in Chapter 9.

Although there are lots of techniques promoted as being good for teaching English learners, teachers are often unsure about how they apply to their own classroom and in what combination they should be used for best results. One of the reasons we created the SIOP® Model was that we wanted to provide teachers with a concrete, systematic way to make learning activities and interaction with English learners understandable and effective.

Currently used in all fifty states in the U.S. and in numerous countries, the SIOP® Model is an empirically validated way of teaching children who are learning a second language at the same time they are learning new concepts, skills, and information in that new language. The SIOP® Model was not originally designed for pre-K classrooms, but given the wide interest, we have undertaken a description of how it can be applied to working with younger children in that setting. In early childhood education (ECE) settings, some of the features of the SIOP® Model may be adjusted from the way they are implemented in elementary and secondary settings because of the unique learning needs of young children. This means that some of the features that focus on academic knowledge or educational background may be redefined for the pre-K child. In those particular cases, we will explain the application to those young learners (see Chapters 4–7).

The SIOP® Model: 8 Components and 30 Features

The SIOP® Model is composed of thirty features grouped into eight components essential for making content comprehensible for English learners: Lesson Preparation, Building Background, Comprehensible Input, Strategies, Interaction, Practice & Application, Lesson Delivery, and Review & Assessment. A full explanation of each component and feature, including the theoretical and research background as well as practical applications, can be found in *Making Content Comprehensible for Elementary English Learners: The SIOP® Model* (Echevarria, Vogt & Short, 2010a). Appendix A in this book includes a checklist of the SIOP® features and may be particularly useful for planning lessons with young learners. Appendix B includes the comprehensive and abbreviated forms of the SIOP® protocol. By considering the indicators of the protocol, you can begin to understand how closely a lesson might meet the features of the SIOP® Model.

The following discussion provides an overview of the model as teachers would use it for preschool learning activities or kindergarten lessons. Please refer to the SIOP® features in Appendix A as you read through the discussion of each component.

Lesson Preparation

As teachers plan lessons to meet the needs of their students, they develop language and content objectives linked to state curriculum standards. These objectives are shared daily with students and presented in a child-friendly form (see Chapter 4 for examples of content and language objectives). In this way, students know what they are expected to learn and can take an active part in assessing their own progress. Tara Paul, district Curriculum Director, says the following about preschoolers and objectives: "The students really understand that the objectives are their 'job' and what they are going to do with the activity. Every day both content and language objectives are written, 'Today I will....' This is a consistent way to help the students learn those key words." (Tara's program is described in Chapter 8.) Through SIOP® lessons, students gain important experience with content and skills as they progress toward proficiency in their second language. Teachers include supplementary materials, such as picture books, models, real objects, and hands-on and computer-based resources to improve comprehensibility. Sometimes teachers adapt the content or the task depending on the students' background knowledge and level of English proficiency. In early childhood programs, less adaptation may be needed than in secondary schools, for example, because native English speakers and English learners are still acquiring basic proficiency with language. Planned activities must be meaningful, and they need to prepare English learners for elementary school by giving them practice with the academic language, tasks, and topics they will encounter.

Building Background

Effective SIOP® lessons connect new concepts with the students' personal experiences and previous learning, usually involving their home and families. The SIOP® Model underscores the importance of building a broad vocabulary base for students to develop preliteracy skills, the foundation needed to eventually be effective readers, writers, speakers, and listeners. Key vocabulary is taught within the context of learning activities and play. Also, songs and games are used to teach word structures, word families, and word relationships. Songs and chants help with pronunciation and intonation, too. Learning activities should provide opportunities for students to use this vocabulary orally.

Comprehensible Input

Accomplished SIOP® teachers use sheltered and ESL techniques to make content comprehensible, including:

- demonstrations and modeling
- gestures, pantomime, and role-play

- visual aids such as illustrations, real objects, video, and other media
- restating, repeating, and reducing the speed of the teacher's presentation
- previewing important information, and
- hands-on, experiential activities.

SIOP® teachers adjust their speech to the students' proficiency levels and explain academic tasks clearly using visuals and models. In the vignette at the beginning of the chapter, at the very least, Miss Lawrence should have shown the children a completed model of a picture of water colored to indicate water pollution. She could have used simple phrases such as *dirty water* to describe the picture. Perhaps then children would have known what she wanted them to do with the picture.

Strategies

The SIOP® Model calls for explicit instruction and practice in learning strategies. It is important to teach young children learning strategies so they can acquire and reflect on information themselves. Young children are using strategies all the time as they learn new words and figure out how to put sentences together. Teachers and parents do not always articulate and explain the strategies, however. To help students become more independent learners, teachers using the SIOP® Model also scaffold instruction by initiating instruction at the students' current performance level and providing support to move them to a higher level of understanding. See Chapter 5 for more examples for implementing the Strategies component.

Interaction

Students learn through interaction with one another and with their teachers. They need extensive oral language practice to develop vocabulary and to learn more about lesson concepts. Teachers provide models of appropriate speech, word choice, intonation, and fluency, but student–student interaction is also important and needs to occur regularly so English learners can practice using language in a variety of ways for various purposes (see Chapter 3 for more discussion of language uses). Teachers should keep in mind that young English learners acquire language rather easily from native English speaking peers. The interaction features remind teachers to encourage elaborated speech, to group students appropriately for language and content development (sometimes by age, other times by language proficiency), and to provide sufficient wait time for students to process questions and answers in their new language. Furthermore, teachers should allow students to use their native or home language in order to express themselves or to assist them with comprehension.

Practice & Application

Practice and application of new material is critical for all learners. Our SIOP® Model research found that lessons with hands-on, visual, and other kinesthetic tasks benefit English learners because students practice the language and content knowledge through multiple modalities. Effective SIOP® lessons, therefore, include a variety of activities that encourage students to practice and apply not only the content they are learning but also their language skills. It is important for lessons to begin to build literacy skills by linking reading, writing, listening, and speaking skills together.

Lesson Delivery

Successful delivery of a SIOP® lesson means that the content and language objectives were met, the pacing was appropriate, and the students had a high level of engagement. The art of teaching and classroom management skills play a role in effective lesson delivery. Having routines; making sure students know where materials are, what they are expected to do, and what the lesson objectives are; and designing meaningful activities that appeal to children are important factors in the success of the lesson.

Review & Assessment

Each SIOP® lesson or learning activity should wrap up with dedicated time for review. English learners need to revisit key vocabulary and concepts, and teachers should use frequent comprehension checks and other informal assessments to measure how well students retain the information. Accomplished SIOP® teachers also offer multiple pathways for students to demonstrate their understanding. Young learners may use oral language, pictures, and movement to show what they know.

Research-Validated Approach

The SIOP® Model described in this book is the product of several research studies conducted since the early 1990s. A description of the solid and growing research base that shows how the SIOP® Model positively impacts student achievement is seen in Appendix C. The SIOP® Model is grounded in the professional literature and in the experiences of the researchers and participating teachers who worked collaboratively in developing the observation instrument. The theoretical underpinning of the model is that language acquisition is enhanced through meaningful use and interaction.

Today, schools and districts that serve English learners have been informed that they should utilize programs that are "scientifically-based," namely those with research evidence of student success. Although there are a variety of research-based techniques that are effective with English learners (August & Shanahan, 2006), few comprehensive interventions designed specifically for English learners have collected, analyzed, and published achievement data on English learners to date. That is why the SIOP® Model offers such promise. In the national research study for the Center for Research on Education, Diversity & Excellence (CREDE), students who had teachers in content classes who had been trained in the SIOP® Model performed significantly better on a standardized state academic writing assessment than a comparison group of similar students whose teachers had not been trained in the model (Echevarria, Short & Powers, 2006). Subsequent studies have shown that the SIOP® Model has had a positive impact on English learner achievement as well (see Appendix C). Further, there is research support for the individual features of the SIOP® Model (August & Shanahan, 2006).

SIOP® Professional Development

In our extensive work with teachers, we have found that high-quality professional development is critical for improving instruction for English learners—and for all children. Although sometimes teachers prefer to pick and choose among their favored

FIGURE 1.2   *Off to a Good Start*

86% of third grade students who began in Alston's full-day SIOP® kindergarten program in fall 2001 performed at or above grade level on third grade state assessments.

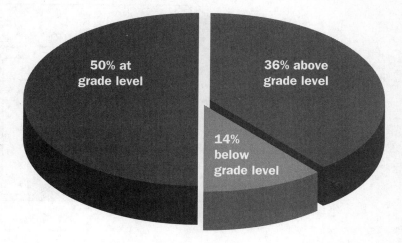

techniques and strategies, research has demonstrated that such practice is ineffective. When implemented consistently as a whole, the features of the SIOP® Model have been shown to improve the achievement of English learners; they are not as effective when they are used selectively or occasionally (Echevarria, et al., 2010a; Echevarria, Short & Powers, 2006; Short, Fidelman & Louguit, in press).

In one school, Lela Alston Elementary, the SIOP® Model was used for ongoing school-wide professional development, beginning in the 2002–03 school year. The school served approximately 400 Latino children in grades K–3. Ninety-seven percent of the children received free or reduced price lunch and 74% were limited English proficient. The commitment to high levels of implementation of the SIOP® Model by having teachers learn SIOP® components one at a time, then observing and coaching teachers led to impressive results. Eighty-six percent of third grade children who began in Alston's full-day kindergarten were performing at or above grade level by Grade 3, seen in Figure 1.2. Figure 1.3 shows children's steady growth from year to year on the state standardized test. On these measures, Alston children outperformed schools with similar demographics across the state (Echevarria, Short & Vogt, 2008).

If you are a teacher, you may begin using the SIOP® Model as a guide to teaching your English learners more effectively. You may want to assess your areas of strength and those that need improvement. As you consider your self-assessment, you may decide to focus on one component at a time. For example, if you are unfamiliar with comprehensible input techniques, you may want to read about them and practice implementing them as a first step. Or, you may need to become accustomed to writing content and language objectives (see Chapter 4) and the way those objectives influence learning activities. As your proficiency in implementing one component of the SIOP® Model is attained, other components of the Model should be added to your teaching repertoire. You might want to use the SIOP® lesson plan checklist in Appendix A as a way to reflect on your teaching.

FIGURE 1.3 *Alston School, 2002–04*

Arizona's Instrument to Measure Standards (AIMS) Test Scores during SIOP® Implementation

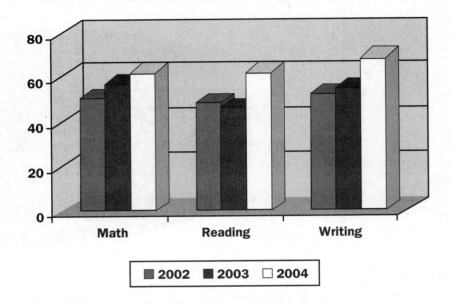

We highly recommend that you begin some form of study of the SIOP® Model to develop a deeper understanding of the needs of English learners and the kind of practices you can use to enhance children's growth across all domains. You might begin a book study with colleagues, or form a professional learning group in which you discuss ideas for lessons, try them out, debrief the outcome, and even observe one another and provide feedback using the SIOP® checklist. Perhaps the SIOP® Model is being used by other teachers with older children in your school or district and you can attend their inservice trainings. The point is that collaboration is the key to professional growth.

A number of school districts have conducted evaluations on their implementation of the model. See *Implementing the SIOP® Model Through Effective Professional Development and Coaching* (Echevarria, Short & Vogt, 2008) for district information and specific ideas for professional development.

Since high-quality early childhood programs contribute to positive outcomes for children, including improved school readiness, higher academic achievement, lower dropout rates, higher high school graduation rates, and higher rates of college attendance (NAEYC, 2009), it is important that teachers implement the features of the SIOP® Model consistently so that we can offer the most appropriate instructional setting possible for young English learners.

The features of the SIOP® Model mirror recommended practice for teaching all young children and reflect many of the Guidelines for Developmentally Appropriate Practice of the National Association for the Education for Young Children (NAEYC, 2009). In fact, NAEYC's position statement says, "Teachers also need to have at the ready a well-developed repertoire of teaching strategies to employ for different purposes" (p. 8). The features of the SIOP® Model provide just such a repertoire—one that is coherent and systematic.

Concluding Thoughts

As you reflect on this chapter and how the SIOP® Model relates to pre-K classrooms, remember the following important points:

- The SIOP® Model is a research-validated approach for teaching English learners.
- The features of the SIOP® Model reflect recommended practice and provide the repertoire of teaching techniques called for by the National Association for the Education for Young Children (NAEYC).
- Professional development enhances effective teaching practice.
- When implemented consistently as a whole, the features of the SIOP® Model have been shown to improve the achievement of English learners; they are not as effective when they are used selectively or occasionally.

chapter 2

Getting to Know Young English Learners and Early Childhood Programs

As educators, we know how important it is to understand the learning needs of young English learners (ELs), as well as their educational backgrounds and personal experiences. This is especially important because the cultural and linguistic diversity of the U.S. population will continue to increase over the next decades (Federal Interagency Forum on Child and Family Statistics, 2010). This diversity presents many challenges, including how to provide high-quality early care and education services to young children who come from non-English speaking homes. These children are acquiring both their home language and English from school and the wider community, either simultaneously or sequentially (Roberts, 2008; Tabors, 2008). Like all children, ELs need quality pre-K experiences to prepare them for school. Our intent in this chapter is to familiarize you with some of the issues associated with educating young ELs so that we can provide the kind of learning experiences these children need and deserve.

Young Children and How They Grow

As we consider the learning needs of all young children, including ELs, we need to consider unique aspects of the early childhood period. First, young children are very dependent on their parents and caregivers. The interactions children have with their caregivers set the stage for learning and growth. When young children receive affection, attention, encouragement, and cognitive stimulation, they generally learn more quickly. These positive experiences lay the foundation for positive development across domains, success in school, and beyond as young learners reach adulthood (Shonkoff & Phillips, 2000; United Nations Children's Fund, 2010). Our job as early childhood educators is to provide developmentally appropriate programs and to support parents in nurturing their children and helping them achieve positive outcomes.

A second unique aspect is that young children's development in one area is intimately intertwined with development in other areas. When we design interventions or teaching strategies to promote language growth, we need to simultaneously support young children's social/emotional, cognitive, and physical development. These, in turn, support further language growth. For example, when young children feel safe and trust their caregivers, they are more likely to take risks while trying to communicate using words in the new language. When children have fun playing physical games, they have a reason to converse with peers in the new language. Children who are learning one language or several languages (either simultaneously or sequentially) follow similar general developmental processes.

Effective teaching approaches for preschool children are grounded in an understanding of development. Three-year-olds are starting to become independent as they leave toddlerhood. Therefore, they need opportunities to explore their world with the support of warm and understanding adults (Charlesworth, 2004). By the age of 3, children have an average vocabulary of 1,000 words, and typically form sentences of 3-5 words. They can answer "if" and "what" questions, such as "What do we use forks for?" These children interact more with peers than do younger children and use more sophisticated language with peers to act out imaginary scenes during dramatic play. Three-year-olds can also follow directions that involve two steps (e.g., "Put the block on the shelf and the bear in the box."). Their gross motor skills have strengthened, so they can run quickly and move around obstacles, jump and land on both feet, ride and steer wheeled toys, and throw and catch balls. Their fine motor skills have increased too, so they can build with small blocks and copy simple figures (Allen & Cowdery, 2009).

Once children reach the age of 4 years, they strive for even more independence from caregivers in play, although they still seek adult approval and assistance when needed (Charlesworth, 2004). Their motor skills have advanced, so they can walk up and down stairs alternating feet, hop on one foot, and turn somersaults. Their fine motor skills have improved too, so they can cut on a line with scissors and print a few capital letters (Allen & Cowdery, 2009). Children at this age engage with peers in more complex dramatic play that has realistic story lines. Between the ages of 4 and 5 years, the average length of the sentences children use is slightly longer (4–5 words), and their vocabularies have increased to about 1,500 words. They can name basic colors and shapes, and can group objects by shape or function. They can also answer simple questions about stories they have heard or that were read to them (Allen & Cowdery, 2009). These are good foundational skills for reading comprehension. They demonstrate more self-confidence, and this is often shown by their asking a lot of questions (Child Development Institute, n.d.).

Five-year-olds show their readiness for kindergarten by feeling self-assured, being very concerned with following rules, and accepting more responsibility (Child Development Institute, n.d.). They are able to count to 10 and to sort objects according to more than one attribute (e.g., color and shape). By this age, they are more likely to keep consistent friendships over time and to play games that require group decisions and rules. When children start kindergarten, the average length of their sentences has increased to 5–6 words and their vocabularies have grown to a range of 2,000–5,000 words (Beck & McKeown, 1996). Although their vocabularies and sentence complexity continue to grow, by this age, children are using almost adult-like grammar when speaking (American Speech-Language-Hearing Association, n.d.; Allen & Cowdery, 2009). Thus, they have the right ingredients to develop reading and writing skills in their home language.

English Learners in Early Care and Education

Like all pre-K children, ELs are also acquiring language skills. They, too, are growing their vocabularies, increasing the average length of their sentences, and learning grammatical rules. However, ELs face the additional challenge of developing these language skills in both their home language and English. As teachers, we need to learn about who these children are and understand the particular hurdles they face in learning English.

Many of our young ELs have immigrant parents or are immigrants themselves. As a result, they tend to speak a language other than English at home and so have limited exposure to English until they are in school. A recent count found that over 37 million U.S. residents are foreign born. Most of them are Hispanic (48%), followed by Asian (23%), White (21%), and Black (8%) immigrant populations (Camarota, 2007). Since 1972, the percentage of school-age children from racially and ethnically diverse backgrounds has doubled (National Center for Education Statistics [NCES], 2009). And, among the school-age population, 79% of children who speak a home language other than English speak Spanish (Garcia, Kleifgen, & Falchi, 2008).

Although a large portion of ELs (61%) are concentrated in six states: California, Arizona, Texas, New York, Florida, and Illinois, every state educates ELs (United States Department of Education, 2010). Moreover, in recent years, states that previously had low EL populations have seen vast increases in the number of school children from non-English speaking homes. For example, between 1995 and 2005, the EL populations in North and South Carolina, Kentucky, Tennessee, Indiana, Nebraska, South Dakota, and Colorado more than tripled (Garcia et al., 2008). This has generated a need for educational programs different than those of twenty years ago.

Consider the five states with the fastest growing Hispanic populations in the past decade: Arkansas, Georgia, South Carolina, North Carolina, and Tennessee (United States Census Bureau, 2006). These states are now considered "new gateways" for immigrants because so many foreign-born individuals choose to settle in these areas (Singer, 2004). These first generation immigrants are entering into predominantly English speaking communities, with few supports in place for non-English speaking individuals. First generation immigrants are likely to struggle with financial stability as well as with English language skills. In particular, Hispanic immigrants are more likely to live in poverty, speak poor English, and have less well educated parents than those who are native born (Fry & Passel, 2009). Non-English speaking children who live in traditional majority English speaking communities face challenges when appropriate teacher training, program designs, and instructional materials are not in place.

Conversely, California and Texas, with the largest number of ELs and Hispanic inhabitants, have immigrant populations that are increasing more slowly. These states have a high percentage of second and third generation Hispanics. These individuals tend to live in established Hispanic communities and likely have lived there for an extended period of time. Yet, second and third generation Hispanics also face challenges. Specifically, Hispanics who have been living in the United States for three generations or more are more likely to live in single parent households, which often implies reduced household income levels, and are more likely to experience health problems (Fry & Passel, 2009).

Teachers of English Learners

As the number of culturally and linguistically diverse children in the United States increases rapidly, the need for teachers who are skilled at educating these children also increases. We know how important it is that teachers create optimal learning environments for ELs so that they become well educated adults, ready to contribute to the economy and support their families (National Task Force on Early Childhood Education for Hispanics, 2007). Yet while aiming for this long-term goal, teachers confront significant pressure to meet the accountability demands of the federal No Child Left Behind legislation (NCLB, 2001). NCLB requires states to set goals for student progress in English language development and in certain content areas yearly. If students fail to meet the goals, schools may face funding cuts or other sanctions (United States Department of Education, 2010).

To meet the NCLB federal mandate and prepare ELs for a productive life in the United States, teachers need to have the necessary skills to communicate competently with all children and their families (Barrera & Corso, 2002), foster English language development among all children, and teach content knowledge to the entire class (Antunez, 2002). Unfortunately, teachers who have all these skills are not easy to find. Of schools (public and private) that have vacancies in teaching positions, one-third report vacancies in English as a Second Language (ESL) positions (NCES, 2003-04). As a result, the responsibility for teaching ELs often is placed on the shoulders of mainstream teachers, many of whom have not had adequate preparation. While over half of teachers have ELs in their classrooms, less than one-fifth feel prepared to work with these students. In fact, more than 50% of teachers report never having received any training for working with ELs. This statistic is even more overwhelming for rural areas, which often are now the "new gateways" for immigrants with very limited English language skills. Over three-fourths (83%) of rural teachers report never having received any training to meet the needs of this population of students (NCES, 2002).

The fact that many teachers feel unprepared to meet the needs of ELs is alarming, especially when researchers tell us that teaching these children requires additional skills beyond those for teaching children whose first language is English (Adger, Snow & Christian, 2002; United States Department of Education, 2010). These additional skills include knowledge of the process and stages of second language acquisition, cultural norms and their effects on teacher-child and peer relationships, the role of first language and culture in building knowledge, and the ways in which the United States's educational system affects culturally and linguistically diverse children (Clair & Adger, 1999). Teachers also need to know strategies and techniques that integrate language learning with content learning (Echevarria & Graves, 2010; Heritage, Silva & Pierce, 2007). Without these additional skills, many teachers struggle to teach English learners.

Challenges in Early Childhood Instruction with English Learners

While teachers are committed to providing quality learning experiences and helping young children's development, their underpreparation can limit their ability to meet some of their students' learning needs. The number and types of challenges may differ by classroom, program, or state; however, some challenges tend to be shared. These include maintaining day-to-day communication with children and their families, procuring necessary resources, and obtaining effective training to serve young ELs.

The purpose of this book is to provide educators with just such a resource, one that can be used for effective training of teachers of ELs. By presenting the SIOP® Model to early childhood educators, we offer a way to make instruction understandable for ELs while at the same time developing their English language skills. The SIOP® Model organizes recommended practices for teaching young children in ways that provide teachers with practical strategies to meet the needs of ELs, as well as children with a variety of diverse needs. As you can see in Figure 2.1, the SIOP® Model envelops the skills children bring, the standards that guide program implementation, the strategies teachers use, and the activities that children do.

Communicating with families is important for sharing information and building collaborative relationships so teachers and parents can work together to support children's learning and development (Coltrane, 2003; Gándara, Maxwell-Jolly, & Driscoll, 2005; Worthington, et al., 2010). More and more schools employ bilingual teachers, paraprofessionals, or other staff members to help address this challenge, but the demand is often greater than the bilingual staff members can meet. This is not unique to one geographic area; programs across the U.S. report having difficulty finding and retaining skilled bilingual staff. As a result, teachers often resort to using gestures and pictures to communicate with families, as well as using young children, themselves, as interpreters. While these strategies are not ideal, nor are they always effective, parents recognize that teachers care about collaborating on their children's development and learning.

FIGURE 2.1 *SIOP® Model Organizes Effective Teaching and Learning Activities*

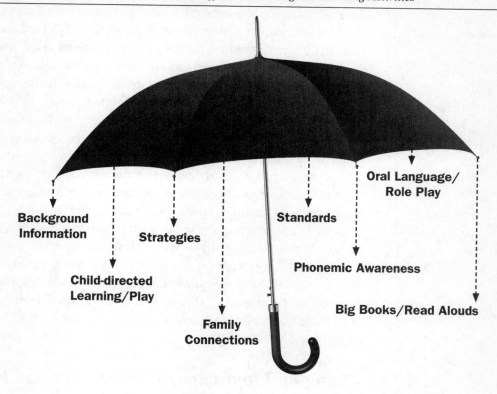

Program administrators who seek to address this communication challenge may want to consider providing more professional development about serving diverse learners. While many programs offer introductory training, teachers need more advanced learning in order to develop the skills necessary to communicate effectively with ELs and their families (Worthington, et al., 2010). For example, teachers might participate in professional development activities to learn some words and phrases in the language that children in their programs speak. While this type of training will not make teachers proficient in the language, it may help build working relationships by showing families that teachers are genuinely interested in collaborating with them.

In a related matter, teachers also report needing assistance in translating materials for parents into their home languages. This is particularly challenging for programs that serve children from a large variety of linguistic backgrounds because the programs may not have access to translators who are skilled at translating into all the various languages spoken by the children, or they may not have time to do so. As a result, official letters may be translated into one or a few languages, but the more frequent informal notes between teachers and parents are not.

Another challenge for teachers serving young ELs is gaining access to necessary instructional resources, especially materials for the children to use, such as books in their native language, bilingual books, or toys that reflect their language and culture. Sometimes this situation occurs because the early childhood program has limited funds for such purchases and sometimes because the home languages are less common and such materials are hard to find.

The final challenge we will discuss here is the lack of professional preparation (inservice training and preservice education) many teachers experience. Practicing teachers need ongoing professional development about the characteristics of young ELs, and effective teaching and assessment practices. They need professional materials (books and videos) to serve as references and models. Although many early childhood education training programs emphasize individualizing instruction to meet the developmental needs of each child, they fail to provide additional information about the specific learning needs of ELs such as those discussed throughout this book. As an unfortunate result, preservice teachers enter the workforce unprepared to provide quality education services to ELs.

Teachers' professional development needs will vary widely. Some will need introductory training to understand general needs of young ELs, and others will need more advanced guidance about specific assessment and teaching practices. Staff working in public schools may have different needs from those working in other early childhood settings. In addition, local community factors (e.g., geographic location, number of support resources or agencies designed to help, immigration trends) may influence the type of challenges faced. As program administrators plan professional development, they need to consider the learning and support needs of staff members who work with children and offer training at various skill levels (Worthington et al., 2010).

Changing Landscape of Early Care and Education

Because children's early experiences set the foundation for subsequent learning, the importance of early developmental education of all children has been recognized by families, educators and social service providers, policy makers, and the general public (Fuller, 2007; Shonkoff & Phillips, 2000). High-quality pre-K experiences, especially for children from low SES families, have been related to enhanced school achievement (Peisner-Feinberg, et al., 2001), as well as positive adult outcomes (Schweinhart, Montie, Xiang, Barnett, Belfield, & Nores, 2005).

High-quality pre-K education is viewed as an economic development tool as well. Education and highly developed skills are central for the success of today's global economy, in which the talents of our nation's entire population are needed. Thus, early childhood education programs are advocated as an effective investment in economic productivity (Heckman & Masterov, 2007; Rolnick & Gruenwald, 2003), and government intervention to enhance the quality of early care and education, especially for children in low-income families, is advocated as a means to ensure quality-of-opportunity goals (Vandell & Wolfe, 2000).

Given the increasing cultural and linguistic diversity among young children in the United States and the importance of early childhood programs, we need to push for high-quality educational services. At present, early care and education is delivered through a patchwork of agencies that frequently have different goals, funding sources, and enrollment criteria. Children participate in center-based child care, family child care programs, and relative care; as well as Head Start and state or locally funded pre-K programs. The majority of child care available in the United States, however, is considered mediocre at best (Helburn et al., 1995; Kontos, Howes, Shinn, & Galinsky, 1995; NICHD Early Child Care Research Network, 2000).

During the 2008–2009 school year, states spent more than $5 billion to enroll 1.5 million pre-K children, but only 16 states met 10 benchmarks for quality standards (Barnett, Epstein, Friedman, Sansanelli, & Hustedt, 2009). Obviously, access to high-quality early care and education experiences cannot be taken for granted.

Widespread efforts to enhance the quality of early care and education settings have been undertaken. For example, the focus on school readiness skills has increased attention to early learning standards, early childhood teacher training and licensure, and pre-K curriculum (Scott-Little, Cassidy, Lower, & Ellen, 2010; Tout & Maxwell, 2010). What we need more of, however, is early childhood educators who are well prepared to teach the diverse learners in their programs and to make learning fun as well as educational. This book represents our small contribution to that effort.

Concluding Thoughts

As the number of ELs increases throughout the U.S. education system, the need for better knowledge and skills to address their learning needs is also increasing. Teachers of young ELs are looking for guidance to provide programming that is developmentally and individually appropriate.

- Early childhood is a unique developmental period, and children are developing skills rapidly.
- Young children develop skills across developmental domains simultaneously.
- All young children need support for language development.
- Young ELs face unique challenges as they are learning multiple languages.
- Increasing attention and resources are being directed to early care and education programs, but there is still much work to do to provide quality early childhood education to all children.
- There is a need for professional development around issues in the education of English learners.

chapter 3

Language Development in Young English Learners

The term *English learners* is somewhat of a misnomer when it applies to young bilingual children because they are learning *language*, not just English. Also referred to as *dual language learners* (Castro, et al., 2010), these children are learning their home language at the same time they are learning English.

The importance of the development of children's language in natural ways cannot be overemphasized. Language is the basis for thinking, reasoning, learning, and communicating, as well as for developing literacy skills. When you think about it, nearly everything we do involves language: thinking about something, talking to friends and family, getting information in person or on the Internet, reading for pleasure, and so forth. Language is the basis for all these activities. When teachers use the SIOP® Model to guide their lessons, children are provided with rich opportunities to use language in a variety of important ways.

How Is Language Learned?

We make the point about learning language in "natural ways" because children will learn language by having opportunities to use it, experiment with it, try out new forms, and discuss topics of interest. Children learn language through all of the following means.

- *Play.* Language and academic skills are embedded in play. Through play, students develop problem-solving, critical thinking, and social abilities in a safe, risk-free environment. Some children who would be shy or inhibited during class discussions—especially English learners—use language freely while playing alone, with peers, or with toys such as puppets. Free Choice time offers children the opportunity to play in the house area, art area, science area, dress-up area, and building area (with blocks and Legos®), or with toys. During these play times, English learners can use their new language with English-speaking peers in a risk-free setting. Participating with others in play allows for exchanging ideas, talking about pretend situations like cooking or cleaning, and using props to stimulate discussion. Teachers mingle among the children during play time asking questions, eliciting language, providing a language model, and nurturing their attempts at expressing themselves.

- *Engaging in stimulating talk.* Children need practice using new words, stringing them together into sentences, asking questions, and learning the way people talk together, such as taking turns speaking. Young children need to hear and practice words orally. It is through this practice with speaking and listening that children expand their language abilities. To promote discussion, teachers choose topics of interest to young learners. For English learners, topics of interest for which new vocabulary is needed are particularly beneficial for language development.

- *Hearing books read aloud.* Interesting stories that are meaningful to the children offer exposure to a multitude of new vocabulary items, including words that are part of the academic language needed for school. Teachers read chunks of text, pause, and then talk about what happened and what the children see in the illustrations, how the story relates to their own lives or experiences, what they think will happen next, and so forth. Rereading the same book multiple times is like listening to a favorite song. There is a comfort in its familiarity, and children will learn more vocabulary if they have multiple exposures to the words.

- *Repetition and imitation.* Some of children's first attempts at communicating are imitations of what they have heard repeatedly, such as *ba-ba* (bottle) and *da* (dog). Throughout their childhood and beyond, young learners will continue to listen to words and expressions they hear frequently and repeat them until they become part of their language repertoire. English learners especially need repeated exposure to academic terminology since language is developed through repetition and imitation.

- *Explicit teaching.* Some aspects of language may not be picked up incidentally by children and will require direct teaching. For example, alphabet songs and games may not provide sufficient exposure for all children to learn the letters of the alphabet. Of course, all children learn at different rates, so care must be taken not to force children to master a skill prematurely. However, explicit teaching may be beneficial when it appears a child is not catching on and will be significantly behind peers when entering kindergarten or first grade. Let's use an alphabet example. Perhaps toward the end of the pre-K year, after a significant amount of time had been spent on learning the alphabet, several children still know only a handful of letters. The teacher would then teach more explicitly to that group, perhaps by using the names of five friends to identify letters in the names. By referring to something familiar, teachers help children make connections to abstract concepts such as letters of the alphabet. In this example, the teacher would then provide more directed activities to practice the letters, such as having students contort their bodies or arms into the letter shapes, labeling objects in the room with the initial letters being studied, and similar activities. If the same letters are in the children's home language, connections can be made to words in their language that begin with those letters.

As children develop language in both their home language and English, they learn to use it in specific ways for specific purposes.

Language Register

We use language in both formal and informal ways; in linguistics this is referred to as *register*. When talking with colleagues about your students, you may refer to them as *kids* but would use the more formal term, *student* or *child*, when writing a report or a letter to parents. Children begin learning from a very young age that a different style of language is used in different situations and with different people. However, they need practice in developing a variety of registers. Youngsters need opportunities to learn about speaking and listening in many different social and academic settings, including in play groups with peers, in school and neighborhood locations with adults, in front of the whole class during a group discussion, and in small groups. For preschoolers, imaginative play in the sandbox or home area provides the chance for a great deal of talking among peers: "We're making a cake. Put water in and stir it up" as well as talking to oneself as play is acted out alone. When working in a small group learning activity, children are exposed to a different register as the teacher uses academic vocabulary and accurate grammar. For kindergarteners, talk in academic settings around, for instance, informational text or math lessons is encouraged. Therefore, multiple opportunities to practice talking in both formal and informal settings with a variety of people should be provided as these children are still in the process of developing language registers.

Language Purposes

In addition to using a variety of styles of language depending on the audience and setting, we also use language for different purposes. Young children use language for some of these reasons:

- To express needs: "More water."
- To give information: "I went to the mall."

- To make predictions: "Maybe the prince will come."
- To persuade others: "Sit down here."
- To form relationships with others: "You're my friend."
- To express opinions, feelings, and point of view: "I like doggies."
- To think, teach, and learn: "A penguin walks slowly but a mouse is fast."

Children already use language for many of these purposes by the time they are 3 years old (Resnick & Snow, 2009). As you can see, nearly all these purposes for using language involve others. Humans are fundamentally social creatures, and we learn by interacting with others. That is one of the reasons that providing lots of opportunity for children to talk is essential in early childhood education settings.

Teacher Roles in Language Development

As mentioned, babies learn language and use it for a variety of purposes from a very young age. As teachers, we need to help children continue to develop language to communicate. Effective communication skills impact children's ability to develop good social relationships and contribute to the prevention of behavior problems.

The role of teachers of young children is often to scaffold their language to assist them in expressing themselves (see Chapter 5, SIOP® Feature #14 for a discussion of scaffolding). Consider the following exchange that we observed in a Head Start program. Notice how the teacher assists both students in expressing themselves after a playground disagreement:

JUAN: "Teacher, he hit me."

FERNANDO: "He called me an idiot."

TEACHER: "Why did you say it?"   (Fernando tells her about a problem with the ball.)

TEACHER (to Fernando):   "How does it feel?"

FERNANDO: "Makes me sad."

TEACHER: "So, it made you sad, or angry?"

FERNANDO: (nods affirmatively)

TEACHER: "When you're angry, what can you do?"

FERNANDO: "Stomp my foot."

TEACHER: "Yes, or tell him how you feel."

TEACHER (turns to Juan):   "So, he hit you because he was angry and he didn't have the words." (to Fernando): "Tell him how you feel."

FERNANDO: "I don't like you taking the ball."

TEACHER: "So, use your words next time. Tell him what bothers you but don't call names."

This example involves a social situation, but scaffolding may be even more important during academic discussions since many academic words aren't typically found in the EL children's everyday settings. Teachers then have the responsibility for providing language learning opportunities in ways that will give young children exposure to words and language use that they may not otherwise have.

First (Home) Language Development

The population of children in early childhood education (ECE) programs has become increasingly diverse. The enrollment of culturally and linguistically diverse pre-K children doubled from 20% in 1990 to approximately 40% in 2000 (U.S. Census Bureau, 1990, 2000). For many children, kindergarten is their first exposure to school—and to English. Because it cannot be assumed that all children attended pre-K programs, teachers of kindergarteners must be sensitive to language and cultural issues.

Effective teachers of young English learners are aware of the importance of developing children's first or home language. Linguists and psychologists generally agree that normally developing children reach oral proficiency in their first language by the age of 5. They learn to use their first language in several registers and for the purposes described previously. They also develop vocabulary and acquire rules of grammar. The developmental period for language from 0–5 years confirms that children in ECE programs are still learning their first language and need opportunities to develop it fully as they begin learning English as an additional language.

The advantages of being bilingual are well known (Baker, 2000; Bialystok & Hakuta, 1995). It provides greater communication networks; it offers cognitive advantages in the areas of thinking, brain plasticity, and memory; and it eventually offers increased employment opportunities. In addition, speaking both the language of their family and the language of the school and broader community well is an obvious advantage, one that is critical to children's well-being.

Many researchers encourage the development of home language literacy in young children. If youngsters learn to read text they understand orally, then they won't have to struggle with meaning as well as the act of reading itself. It is recommended that children be introduced to reading through the use of books in their home language that have highly predictable language patterns (Cloud, Genesee & Hamayan, 2009). In this way, their first exposure to text is more meaningful for them and they will be more comfortable with written language.

Use of children's home language in school is an important part of their overall language development and should be encouraged. Even if you don't speak the home language, you should accept children's attempts to communicate and respond in positive, supportive ways (SIOP® Feature #19). You may find other students in the class speak that home language and they can act as interpreters to share the non-English speaking students' ideas. It is also may be beneficial to encourage parents to use the home language—reading stories, having robust discussions, and sharing conceptual knowledge with their children in that language.

English Language Development

As children are introduced to a new language in school (English), teachers use the kinds of practices discussed throughout this book to make English understandable and to value and validate the children's home language and culture.

When young children learn a second language, they apply strategies that are similar to those used to learn their first language. They listen carefully to distinguish sounds, they learn phonological rules, and they learn to use grammar to construct meaning and expression. In addition, as second language learners, English learners may

- *Go through a silent period.* The child is quietly learning and adjusting to a new way of communicating and learning from a few days to a few weeks.
- *Code-switch.* It is normal for a bilingual person to use English and his/her home language interchangeably, sometimes in the same sentence, especially when learning the second language. For example, one may say, "I want to go to la tienda and buy some dulces." This kind of code-switching should be accepted as the child's way of experimenting with language.
- *Use formulaic expressions.* Children learn the way proficient speakers use language and follow suit. Examples of these expressions include, *I'm sorry, Please excuse me, I wanna …* and *I would like to …* Over time, children will rely less on formulaic phrases and develop their own individual expressions.

Academic Language

Young children must be exposed to the kinds of words that they will be expected to use in elementary school. There are many words that they will not encounter in their daily lives, and teachers need to make sure that these words are part of learning activities so that children will become familiar with them. In Figure 3.1 we show a sample of some academic terms required in kindergarten through second grade.

It is reasonable to introduce academic vocabulary through everyday words. For example, children might conduct a simple experiment growing plants in different locations in the classroom (e.g., by the window, in a closet, in a sink holding a half inch of water). The students may talk about what makes the locations different (e.g., sunlight, darkness, water) and the teacher can point out that these are *factors* (or *variables*) and different *environments* that can affect plant growth. As early childhood educators, we do not need to avoid the more academic terms, but we do need to teach them clearly and in context. It is important to remember too that acquiring academic words is not the sole goal, academic language is also needed in school to acquire new knowledge.

FIGURE 3.1 *Academic Language Required in Grades K–2*

English/ Language Arts	Math	Science	History/ Social Studies
title page	coin	cloud	date
describe	addition	ask	education
author	inch	habitat	neighborhood
words	graph	seasons	map
rhymes	circle	collect	flag

Language Assessment

Effective early childhood educators collect information about their students' language abilities from the start. They use this knowledge to plan lessons and activities that will advance the children's English skills. Some programs do this informally with interview and observation checklists, while some are using more standardized assessments. One example was developed by the World-Class Instructional Design and Assessment (WIDA) consortium. It designed assessments to measure the initial English language ability of English learners and to monitor the annual progress of their English language proficiency in grade levels K–12. For younger learners, the Kindergarten W-APT™ is a diagnostic test whose components can be administered to children in pre-K, kindergarten, or first grade, depending on a child's individual circumstances. The results of this screener help teachers know the level of English students have when entering the class. Later in the year, usually the spring, ELs take the ACCESS for ELLs proficiency test to measure progress. Since most children in pre-kindergarten and kindergarten are pre-literate—whether EL or not—only the oral portions (Listening/Speaking) of the assessments would be given then. However, a child who is more advanced, perhaps by the second half of the kindergarten year, could take all four components: Listening, Speaking, Reading, and Writing. Please see the WIDA website for more information: http://wida.wceruw.org.

Parents as Partners

As we know, parents are a child's first and most important teachers. It makes sense, then, that as educators we should partner with parents so that we can be consistent in our practices and expectations related to language and literacy development. The relationship is mutually beneficial. Families of English learners have much to offer, and teachers can provide suggestions to families for increasing literacy practices at home. In Chapter 8 we highlight a program that makes the family-school connection a priority.

While many families of English learners have low literacy levels, they often have rich oral traditions that can provide a foundation for literacy. When partnering with schools, family members share family stories, legends, poems, songs, folktales, and so forth. These oral forms can be written down and read to others, including the children in class. These literacy experiences link the children's personal lives with the classroom and provide teachers with a deeper understanding of how children's background knowledge can be related to the curriculum (Campano, 2007). Teachers, in turn, might provide parents with suggestions for stimulating language use at home (Vogt, 2010), in the home language or English. Following are some ideas for encouraging parents.

- *Have fun with wordless picture books (those with only illustrations).* The child tells the story as he sees it and the parent asks questions. Or the parent might describe the pictures in detail, introducing descriptive vocabulary.
- *Become a storyteller.* Parents share stories about their childhoods, family anecdotes, funny things that have happened, or whatever is entertaining. When possible, parents include familiar story elements such as "Once upon a time…."; "First … then … next … finally …"; "In the end…"; "The end" and describe the characters in the story with interesting words.

- *Involve the child with household tasks.* For example, parents might have children help group the groceries before putting them away. They would talk about and show how to group the soup cans, cereal boxes, dairy products, snack foods, fresh vegetables, and so forth. The items can be re-grouped differently, perhaps according to size; packaging (canned vs. boxed); preparation (fresh vs. frozen); and so forth. The family laundry can be sorted by color (colored or white), or type (shirts, pants, or skirts). These are wonderful opportunities to talk about sorting, saying the name of each item and identifying its characteristics: hard and soft, big and small, metal and paper. The ability to classify is both a reading and a math skill that young children can begin developing at home.

- *Talk about environmental print.* When driving or walking with children around town, parents identify various signs. Research has shown that some of the first words children can read are those from familiar signs and logos, such as "Mc-Donald's," "Dairy Queen," or "Pizza." Children can also look for numbers they know on license plates, street signs, house or store numbers, and billboards.

These are a few of the many ways that parents can provide language and pre-literacy development in fun ways that occur as a regular part of families' everyday lives. Best of all, they don't require a great deal of time and the pay-off is tremendous.

Supporting Children with Disabilities

Most preschools offer services to children already identified as having disabilities. These young children, including English learners with disabilities, learn in much the same ways as typically developing children. However, because children with disabilities may not learn some skills incidentally, instruction will be more teacher-directed. For example, in a special education pre-K class we observed, the morning song activity required the teacher to be more explicit than in the regular education classroom. When it was time for each child to say, "Good morning," the teacher often pointed to her mouth to indicate that it was the child's turn to speak. She said to a child with autism, "Eyes up here; good looking" so that he would make eye contact when speaking. She made movements to the song (clapping, waving) in an animated way because she was modeling actions for the children to imitate. She needed to encourage a number of children individually to participate in clapping, but when a child didn't clap along, she didn't pressure him to do so. The class activities were the same as in any other early childhood classroom, with some accommodations. In making your classroom a productive learning environment for children with disabilities, we offer the following suggestions.

- *Have routines.* Consistent routines help children learn about the classroom environment and the expectations of school. The schedule does not vary much day to day, although the content of the activities does. For English learners, routines make them less dependent on oral instructions and so are easier to follow. Each week the teacher sends home a schedule of a week's activities so that families know the daily routines and can help prepare their child for the week's activities.

- *Give time.* All children learn a little differently from one another, but generally children with disabilities will require more time to complete a task or learn a concept than typically developing children. Make sure that the necessary extra time is planned into learning activities.

- *Break big tasks into smaller tasks.* If a task is too hard and the child needs constant support, make it easier. Following a step-by-step process for teaching skills will yield better outcomes.

- *Repeat, repeat, repeat.* Repetition is key, especially for English learners with disabilities. They are learning a new language at the same time they are learning a lot of new skills, information, and concepts. The cognitive and linguistic load for these children is great; repetition is an effective way of making the message understandable.

- *Use pictures or gestures.* In numerous places throughout this book, we discuss how visuals assist English learners. Also, children respond well to gestures and hand movements, such as air writing (also called finger spelling) letters of the alphabet. These scaffolds help make the abstract more concrete.

- *Pay attention to sensory issues.* Observe where the children are comfortable or uncomfortable and why (e.g., peaceful or noisy, sparse or cluttered, bright or darkened, crowded or uncrowded), which toys they like, whom they tend to sit with. Make adjustments accordingly.

For a complete discussion of learning disabilities and English learners, please see Echevarria & Vogt (2011) *RTI and English Learners: Making It Happen.*

Concluding Thoughts

As you reflect on this chapter and how language development impacts learning, remember the following important points:

- Young children are learning language, both their home language and English, during the early childhood years.

- Classrooms need to provide the kind of environment that stimulates language development through active engagement, lots of opportunities to talk, and abundant ways for children to explore interests and new learning.

- Children's home or first language is a valuable tool that they use to make themselves understood as well as to develop critical language skills that will transfer to their learning of English.

- Families are important assets that teachers and administrators should enlist as partners in the education of their children.

- English learners with disabilities learn in much the same ways as typically developing children. Keep consistent routines and schedules to support their participation. Also, find ways to adjust the environment to assist their learning such as slowing down, reducing the amount of sensory stimulation, and giving them more time to complete tasks.

chapter 4

Using the SIOP® Model with Young Learners: Lesson Preparation and Building Background

In this chapter and the three that follow, we present the SIOP® Model's eight components and 30 features and offer suggestions for using the SIOP® Model with young learners in pre-K and kindergarten. As mentioned in Chapter 1, although the SIOP® Model was not originally developed with pre-K children in mind, we will discuss specific ways that the model can be used effectively for meeting the unique learning needs of very young English learners.

Without question, learning is a primary goal in ECE programs, and the SIOP® Model provides a framework for ensuring that teachers' interactions with English learners will be optimal. When the features of the SIOP® Model are implemented to a high degree, the classroom environment is one that promotes respect for diversity,

fosters cognitive and language development, and focuses on meeting the individual needs of each student.

To be effective, teachers must get to know each child in the group well. An effective teacher interacts with the children individually and in small and large groups, all the while eliciting their ideas as a way to develop language and cognition. (See Chapter 3 for a discussion of language development.) The teacher also pays close attention to student progress and uses assessments such as observation, analysis of student work, and interviews with families as an ongoing part of the teaching and learning experience. He or she uses the information and insights gathered to make plans and adjustments to promote each child's individual development and learning as fully as possible.

Components of the SIOP® Model

In this chapter we will review the first two components, Lesson Preparation and Building Background, followed by a discussion of how the features of these components apply to young learners. In the next three chapters we will follow the same format with the remaining SIOP® components. As you read this chapter and those that follow, keep in mind that although they are discussed individually, the SIOP® Model's features are interrelated and support one another.

Lesson Preparation

As early childhood teachers prepare lessons, also called *learning activities,* they need to keep in mind what research tells us about the way young children develop and learn. For instance, as discussed in detail in Chapter 3, language development is the foundation for literacy, so there is much more emphasis on language development with young learners than on specific academic skill development. While skills are taught, they are done so in a language rich and developmentally appropriate context.

Lesson Preparation Features

1. Content objectives clearly defined, displayed and reviewed with students
2. Language objectives clearly defined, displayed and reviewed with students

---

The first two SIOP® features focus on objectives. They will reflect student learning outcomes, referred to as *standards* in K–12 and increasingly talked about in preschool as well. Illinois is the first state to implement preschool standards, and others may follow. Preschool standards should allow continuity with kindergarten standards, but not at the expense of attention to physical and social-emotional development (Bodrova, Leong, & Shore, 2004).

Although there are a number of modifications that we suggest teachers consider when determining content and language objectives for young children, having objectives is important and is supported by research (August & Shanahan, 2006). Objectives are beneficial for a number of reasons. First, teachers need to have a focus for instruction in order to be more effective. When teachers are cognizant of the lesson's focus, they are more likely to teach the skill or concept during instructional time and to reinforce it during teachable moments throughout the day. Another reason for objectives is for students to know what they are learning. The NAEYC position statement says that indicators of effective early childhood instruction include "Children are active and engaged; the goals are clear and shared by all" (NAEYC, 2003, p. 2).

Many young learners, even some kindergarteners, are not yet readers. The posted objectives are written in child-friendly terms, but have visuals to provide meaning. In the examples provided in Figure 4.1 (on pages 33–35), notice that the first objective is for the teacher to use and is followed by a student-friendly objective presented the way it can be understood by children. If students are learning the concepts of *first, second,* and *last*, the pictures make the objective understandable. When introducing the objective, the teacher might have students stand in a line in groups of three and identify who is first, second, and last in line. The objective may also be reinforced with pictures to illustrate an activity such as snack time; first we line up, second we wash our hands, and last we eat. Classroom features such as cut out construction paper feet taped on the floor in front of the sink where children wait for a turn or approaching a playground slide might also illustrate the objectives of learning that three children standing in a line are in order of first, second, and last.

It is useful for children to see the content and language objectives posted throughout the week as a reminder of the focus of the week's learning. Posted objectives help students to be "clued in" to what they are learning, and they also provide exposure to the written words they will use.

Teachers sometimes have difficulty distinguishing between content and language objectives, especially in early childhood classrooms where much of the content children are learning is language related. (Please see Chapter 8 for an example of how teachers at Roundy Elementary use color coding to distinguish content and language objectives.) Content objectives reflect what the children will learn, such as the one for the lesson in Figure 4.2 on pages 36–37: *Students will identify emotions they feel such as excited and afraid.* The language objective in this lesson provides oral language practice and reinforcement of the content objective: *Students will discuss how to express emotions in a healthy way.* Language objectives promote student academic language growth since academic language is not something children typically encounter in their every day lives. It needs to be explicitly taught in school.

In one school where all teachers use the SIOP® Model, a third grader, Karina, told us that she didn't speak any English when she entered kindergarten, but she added that because of the language objectives on the board, "Well, that's how I got better in English." The evidence of this is anecdotal, but we found it insightful that not only was she aware of the language objectives but she attributed her language growth to them.

Resnick and Snow (2009) discuss several aspects of language—basic linguistics—that children should learn. These may be used as the basis for language objectives. To illustrate these, we have written sample content objectives (CO) from a variety of topics and language objectives (LO) that show how to explicitly teach language through content. The aspects of language are (Resnick & Snow, 2009):

- Phonology: What does it sound like?

  CO: Students will identify the initial sound.

  LO: Students will say the sound aloud to a partner. This language objective gives children individual oral language practice.

- Semantics: What does it mean, and where does it belong?

  CO: Students will group pictures of objects by category (toys, animals, people, clothing).

  LO: Students will state why the picture goes in a particular category. This language objective demonstrates understanding of the relationship among items and gives students oral practice articulating their reasoning skills.

- Syntax: What kind of a word is it?

  CO: Students will name and describe a variety of foods.

  LO: Students will chorally read descriptions and point to the describing word in each one. This language objective provides children practice seeing that describing words, or adjectives, precede a noun when the teacher writes phrases students form while meeting the content objective, such as "the red apple," "the yellow banana." With exposure, children internalize syntactic patterns (Resnick & Snow, 2009).

- Morphology: What is its form and how can it change?

  CO: Students will listen to a story and answer comprehension questions (Where did the dog go? Why was he sad?).

  LO: Students will use past tense in telling their answers about the story. With the teacher's assistance, children have an opportunity to see how past tense forms are used.

- Pragmatics: How is it used?

  CO: Students will tell an addition story using the numbers 1 and 2.

  LO: Students will practice taking turns when telling their math stories. This language objective gives children a chance to practice good pragmatics skills, namely listening to others and taking turns in a conversation.

Also see Chapter 3 for additional aspects of language that provide the basis for language objectives.

In Chapter 8 you will read about the importance of content and language objectives in the ECE programs featured. One teacher, Cathy Fox, says that posting the objectives and reviewing them with the students keeps her focused and also provides the students with a purpose for learning each day. Although she initially found writing objectives challenging, she believes this task has had the greatest positive impact on her instructional practice.

Following are some suggestions about selecting content and language objectives.

- *Objectives should be age appropriate.* Young children are not developmentally ready for abstract concepts, nor should they be expected to sit for extended periods of time listening to the teacher or completing paper-and-pencil tasks. The early school years should be spent engaging in talk about topics of interest to the children and ones that capitalize on their curiosity; listening to books read aloud and talking about them; singing songs that subtly practice pronunciation of words and intonation of phrases; exploring new things; and interacting with peers while playing with interesting and engaging materials. Objectives should reflect these developmentally appropriate activities, which are intended to facilitate cognitive, language, socio-emotional, and physical development. Remember that language learning is a process, and English learners in particular need even more opportunity to practice using new words and hear the new language in natural ways (e.g., listening to books read aloud and talking with peers in real and fantasy play).

- *Objectives should be posted and shared orally with students.* The teacher may model by reading the objectives aloud and pointing to the accompanying pictures. Then students repeat what the teacher has said. As mentioned in the example of first, second, and last, the teacher explains the objectives, gives examples, and elicits background knowledge from the students about the objective. Figure 4.1 shows the teacher's objective, *SW (Students will) match mother animals with their babies using pictures, stuffed animals, animal cards, or animal figurines.* As the teacher shares the objective, she elicits language by asking students to name the various animals, tell if they have ever seen one, and so forth. This also activates their prior knowledge, a feature of building background discussed later.

- *Objectives should be displayed pictorially.* As mentioned previously, there is value in environmental print, but with young children, particularly those less proficient in English, objectives are more meaningful if they are presented in a way that is understandable. A variety of forms may be used such as pictures with labels or simple sentences, or, for older children, complete sentences including using *SW* (*students will*). Figure 4.1 shows samples of objectives from various subject areas. As you can see, objectives vary in their level of complexity depending on the students' age, developmental level, and time of year, as objectives will become more complex across time.

- *Objectives should be addressed in a less formal way than in grades 1–12 classrooms.* Since "instruction" takes many forms with young learners, such as directed play, spontaneous teaching moments, and structured learning opportunities, objectives will focus on a skill or concept that may be woven into the day's activities. In ECE settings, the same objectives may guide learning for several days or for a week. For example, one objective for the week in the lesson seen in Figure 4.2 was to express emotions in a healthy way. During play time, the teacher tells students, "I'm going to the art table if anyone wants to join me." At the table, several students work on a Feeling Book, drawing faces on cards to express a variety of emotions. Over the course of the day, all students worked on a Feeling Book at one time or another. Also, throughout the day the teacher takes opportunities to ask students what they are feeling or how their actions make another student feel. So, the objectives are specific and shared with students, but taught in a less formal way than in elementary and secondary classrooms.

● *Objectives for pre-reading, pre-writing, and oral language lessons may be similar, but should still be separated into language and content goals.* Sometimes the lesson has a language focus and so the content objective will be language-related. For example, an initial phonics lesson may focus on the letter "m." A content objective may be that students recognize the letter "m" in a list of letters. A language objective may be that they pronounce the sound of the letter "m." Another lesson might include having children sound out a word with the letter "m" as the initial sound, which could be a content objective, while having children generate words that begin with the "m" sound could be a language objective. We suggest you not worry too much about distinguishing between content and language objectives in these cases, but maintain the routine of having both types so children are aware of the importance of language and expect both objectives in pre-K lessons and beyond.

● *Objectives should build on one another.* For young learners, objectives often reinforce previous ones so that there is continued reinforcement of skills. When a new objective is introduced that builds on a previous one, the same visuals are used to support children's recall. For example, in Figure 4.1, the first objective introduces the concept of first, second, and last. Later in the year when the concept of prediction is introduced, the same visuals are used so that children recall how to order things. The teacher might summarize what happened first in the story, and then ask the children to predict what will happen next. The consistent visual support assists their recall of ordering as they give their predictions.

Once you have written your content and language objectives, you might use this checklist to evaluate them:

—— The objectives are observable.

—— The objectives are written and presented in language the students can understand.

—— The content objective is related to the key concept of the lesson.

—— The language objective promotes student academic language growth (it is not something most students already do well).

—— The language objective connects clearly with the lesson topic or lesson activities.

—— I have a plan for assessing student progress on meeting these objectives during the lesson.

Lesson Preparation Features

3. Content concepts appropriate for age and educational background level of the children

---

FIGURE 4.1 *Sample Content and Language Objectives*

Preschool and kindergarten teachers need to develop content and language objectives to guide instruction. They think about what children will know and be able to do at the end of a learning activity. Children, of course, cannot read complete sentences so the content and language objectives are posted in student-friendly form. The following examples show objectives for the lesson and the teacher's instruction followed by the same objectives represented in student-friendly form.

Teacher:

CO: Students will (SW) place three objects along a line and respond nonverbally to questions about the order of the objects.

LO: SW tell a partner the position of three objects, using the words first, second, and last.

Point to the pictures of 3 children playing. Ask, *Who is first, second and last?*

Show students objects and place them along a line. Ask, *Which is first, second and last?*

Tell a partner the position of your (object) . Use the words first, second, and last.

_____ *is first.* _____ *is second.* _____ *is last.*

Student-friendly:

First   Second   Last

Teacher:

CO: SW match mother animals with their babies using pictures, stuffed animals, animal cards, or animal figurines.

LO: SW orally share with a partner or in a small group which picture of a baby animal goes with the picture of the mother animal.

Tell a partner which mother goes with each baby animal.

The baby _____ goes with the mother _____ .

The mother _____ goes with the baby _____ .

Student-friendly:

Mother and baby

Teacher:

CO: SW match consonant initial sounds of words to pictures.

CO: SW write letter-like symbols and letters to match pictures.

LO: SW orally name letters.

(continued)

FIGURE 4.1 *Sample Content and Language Objectives* (continued)

Student-friendly:

 B

Teacher:

CO: SW draw objects for a food shopping list.

LO: SW read their lists to a partner.

Write a list for the grocery store. Read it to your partner.

Student-friendly:

List

Apple

Chicken

Teacher:

CO: SW act out a scene to predict what happens next in a story.

LO: SW listen to a story, look at the pictures, and orally. Predict what will happen next.

When teacher stops reading, tell or "predict" what will happen next.

I predict that _____ .

I think that _____ .

Student-friendly:

Think

Tell

First

Second

Last

(continued)

FIGURE 4.1 *Sample Content and Language Objectives* (*continued*)

Teacher:

CO: SW evaluate foods as likes or dislikes.

LO: SW orally state which food they like or dislike.

Place the pictures in the column of like 😀 *or don't like* 🙁 *then use the words to tell a partner what you like and what you don't like.*

Students use the sentence stems: I like _____ . I don't like _____ .

Student-friendly:

Like   Dislike

Food

    When we apply this SIOP® feature to early childhood learners, we recognize that in pre-K, children may not have had prior educational opportunities. Therefore we need to interpret this feature so we consider the children's age and developmental level when choosing content concepts. We know that children develop at various rates and that individual development is often uneven across language domains. Because of this, teaching should match the child's developmental level and be based on assessment information. Briefly, assessment methods used to gather information about each child include observation, a clinical interview (an extended dialogue in which the adult seeks to discern the child's conceptual knowledge or strategic thinking), an examination of the child's work, individual assessments, and discussions with the family (NAEYC, 2009). Once a child's developmental level is determined, instruction is individualized to make it appropriate and meaningful for the child.

Lesson Preparation Features

4. Supplementary materials used to a high degree, making the lesson clear and meaningful

---

    The modifications for this feature are in degree rather than in kind. With students in elementary school, we encourage SIOP® teachers to use supplementary materials rather than rely on paper-and-pencil tasks. With young learners, however, the

FIGURE 4.2 *Adapted from Chanty Lim's Feeling Book Lesson*

SIOP® LESSON PLAN

Class Level: Pre-K
Class Periods: Center Time
Subject: Emotions (Social-Affective Development)

Topic:	Feeling Book
Content Objective:	• SW identify emotions they feel such as excited and afraid
Language Objectives:	• SW discuss how to express emotions in a healthy way
Key Vocabulary:	Feeling, emotion, excited, afraid
Materials:	Card stock paper squares, pencils, marker, mirror, pictures of facial expressions.

SIOP® Features:

Preparation	Scaffolding	Grouping Options
_X_ Adaptation of content	_X_ Modeling	__ Whole class
_X_ Links to background	_X_ Guided practice	_X_ Small groups
__ Links to past learning	_X_ Independent practice	_X_ Partners
__ Strategies incorporated	__ Comprehensible input	_X_ Independent

Integration of Processes	Application	Assessment
__ Reading	_X_ Hands-on	_X_ Individual
_X_ Writing	_X_ Meaningful	__ Group
_X_ Speaking	_X_ Linked to objectives	__ Written
_X_ Listening	_X_ Promotes engagement	_X_ Oral

Resources:

Building Background:	Whole Class—The teacher reads the content and language objectives. She asks the children when they feel happy and when they feel sad. Then she introduces the words *excited* and *afraid*. The teacher gives a personal example, such as "I feel excited when I go to Disneyland." At this point, the goal is to get the words and ideas introduced. If the children are unclear about what a certain emotion is, such as *excited*, simply give an example or show a picture and move on. Conclude the time by singing the song, "If you're happy and you know it…" (stamp your feet, raise your hand, etc)
Presentation:	Small Group—The children create a Feeling Book to illustrate emotions by drawing faces to represent the feeling on cards. The Feeling Book consists of 4 to 5 card stock pages and each card has a blank circle that represents a face, seen in Figure 4.3. The teacher begins by showing a sample Feeling Book to the children. Then she asks each child, "What is a feeling you have sometimes?" A child responds with a word such as *angry*. The teacher asks the child to draw a face that expresses the emotion the child named. If they cannot think of a visual representation of the feeling, the teacher shows the child pictures of angry facial expressions or holds up a mirror to the child's face telling him to make a sad face, for example. When the child completes the drawing, the teacher asks, "What feeling is this?" The child tells the teacher and she writes the word under the face to label the emotion. The teacher discusses with children healthy ways of expressing emotions. She asks, "What should you do when you're angry?" and they discuss ways of expressing anger in healthy ways.

(continued)

FIGURE 4.2 *Adapted from Chanty Lim's Feeling Book Lesson* (continued)

Practice & Application:	When a child has finished drawing 4 or 5 expressions on the cards, she takes each drawing and asks the child, "When do you feel… (sad, happy, afraid, etc)?" Each child is encouraged to answer using a complete sentence. The teacher provides the prompt, "Sometimes I feel (happy, sad, nervous) when…"
Review & Assessment:	The teacher staples the cards together to form a Feeling Book. She reviews each of the feelings with each child. She uses the key words repeatedly throughout the lesson and at the conclusion. The teacher assesses the children's understanding of the key vocabulary and concepts through her discussion with them using their Feelings Books. Throughout the day, the teacher takes opportunities to reinforce the objectives. For example, when children have a conflict about playing with toys, the teacher asks how they feel when _____ happens and how they can express that feeling in a healthy way. If a child says, "I don't like you sitting so close", praise him for using his words to express feelings rather than pushing.
Extension Activities:	The Feelings Book may be used in a number of ways for oral language practice. As a follow-up to the lesson, ask parents to have their child explain his or her book to them (in either language) using the words that express their feelings. Also, in class, children may be asked to retell about their feelings, when they feel a certain emotion, and so forth. They might work with a partner to share their book or with the teacher in a small group. During whole class time, the teacher might review by asking, "Who has a drawing of angry (sad, excited, happy)?" The children show the corresponding drawing.

classroom is filled with books, blocks, puppets, dress-up clothes, props, art supplies, and other manipulatives for counting, categorizing, and so forth. The classroom is organized into multiple learning areas such as a book area; kitchen area; computer area; carpet area for playing with trucks, puzzles, and blocks and for group activities (reading, singing, sharing); discussion corner; music center; and science area.

Each of these areas has supplementary materials that assist with making the learning objectives clear and meaningful. It is important to add new items periodically to stimulate children's interest and maintain their attention. For English learners, visuals and models are especially important to render meaning to what is being discussed or taught. In the lesson involving children creating a Feeling Book of drawings representing emotions, presented in Figure 4.2, the teacher had a sample Feeling Book to show the children. For all children, but particularly for English learners, a model of a completed book or other product is essential so that they can see what the expectation is. Computers provide an opportunity for children to see and hear stories that can be read multiple times for meaning and at the same time expose the listener to models of standard English grammar and pronunciation.

Lesson Preparation Features

5. Adaptation of content to all levels of student proficiency

---

FIGURE 4.3 *Drawn by Sydney L.*

As a part of effective instruction for young learners, teachers adapt what they are teaching to the language proficiency level of each student. For early childhood situations, this feature must be interpreted as adapting the content to the students' developmental level as well. In the lesson in Figure 4.2, you will see that the teacher planned ahead to adapt the content of the lesson for both language proficiency and developmental level.

The teacher asks each child, "What is a feeling you have sometimes?" Some children respond with a word such as *happy*. The teacher then asks a child to draw a face that expresses the emotion the child named. Some children may not be able to identify emotions, so the teacher adapts by showing pictures of people's faces with each one expressing a different emotion. After the pictures stimulate the children's thinking, she asks again, "What is a feeling you have sometimes?" The teacher encourages each child to answer, "Sometimes I feel … (happy, sad, nervous)." Some students will be able to answer with a complete sentence while others will repeat the sentence frame the teacher provides. In drawing a representation of an emotion, some children are capable of naming of an emotion and drawing the expression. For those who can't, the teacher holds a mirror for the child to look into to see his facial expression, for example, a sad face or a nervous face. After drawing an expression and identifying the emotion, the teacher labels the picture (see Figure 4.3), and then asks the child when he feels that emotion. The teacher also asks the paraprofessional to translate when a child is unsure of the directions, if a one is available. The same adaptations are made as children complete the 5 cards. Once the books are completed, they become reading material for the children to use in class or at home.

SIOP® Lesson Preparation Features

6. Meaningful activities that integrate lesson concepts with language practice opportunities for reading, writing, listening, and/or speaking

---

Recent research studies have shown the importance of providing young children with high-quality schooling; this is especially advantageous to low-income minority students (Raudenbush, 2009). One aspect of high-quality teaching is making sure that activities are meaningful to the children and offer an abundance of language practice opportunities, including using language in reading, writing, speaking, and listening. Lessons and activities are made meaningful in a number of ways including:

- *Making language understandable.* Taken literally, an activity is not meaningful if it involves language that the child does not understand. Teachers need to use comprehensible input techniques and also provide verbal scaffolds (see Features #10–12 and 14 in the chapters that follow) to make the message—written or verbal—understandable for English learners. For some of you, the sentence, *¿Qué hacen los maestros cuando los niños no entienden lo que dicen?* would require some scaffolding and clues to be meaningful. Whether spoken or written, the sentence is not understandable to you without some support provided. The same situation occurs throughout the day for English learners. They literally cannot make meaning from what the teacher says or what is written. Sometimes translation is required for the language to be meaningful and in other situations, techniques can be used to make English understandable.

- *Using culturally appropriate activities.* With multiple cultures represented in a class, it may be challenging to integrate each child's specific cultural practices into the activities or lessons. Nevertheless, effective teachers of English learners have sensitivity toward and an appreciation of the children's family and community practices. In SIOP® classes, teachers look for ways to integrate the children's cultures, such as by adding multicultural books to the classroom library. Also, activities are made meaningful when children are encouraged to express their knowledge through drawing and telling stories that reflect their culture and their experiences outside of school. Teachers should celebrate children's contributions and should *never* "correct" a child's expression of his or her culture, regardless of how inadvertent or subtle that correction might be.

- *Following children's interests.* Children are encouraged to self-select activities that are of interest to them rather than having an excessive amount of structured class time or teacher-directed activities. When children are interested in an activity, they are more likely to engage in behaviors that contribute to their own development. Requiring a child to practice a skill yields a much less productive result than providing opportunities for the child to choose from a variety of activities such as reconstructing models, exploring books, or doing an art project that supports the lesson's objective. In one classroom we observed during center time, a child selected a book about Cinderella. The language objective for the week was to discuss how to express emotions in healthy ways. The child looked through the book independently and then attempted to get the attention of two other girls ("look at Cinderella, *mira, mira*, look at my book"). She then went to the paraprofessional and they looked through the book together, speaking mostly in Spanish. The paraprofessional asked questions such as "How do you think he feels? Is she afraid? What do you think she will do? Is that a good idea?" and so forth. After about 10 minutes of interacting with the paraprofessional, the child took the book and said, "I want to go to the book corner to read." She walked toward the book corner, but then went to the house area, grabbed a purse, and went to sit next to the teacher to show her the book. She asked in English, "Which princess do you want to be?" They talked about the book in English, looking at the pictures for approximately 5 minutes. In those 20 minutes, the child's attention was maintained because of her interest in the book. She had opportunities to practice oral language in both English and Spanish, express ideas, identify and discuss emotions (the content and language objectives), identify words, and hear the teacher's and paraprofessional's ideas about the story. A very productive child-directed learning time!

Building Background

In this component, the idea is to build upon children's own background knowledge as we take them to a higher level of understanding or introduce new concepts to them. The National Association for the Education of Young Children (NAEYC, 2009) emphasizes the importance of providing young children with a learning environment that respects their culture and language and fosters their relationship with their families and community. Effective teachers build on what the children bring to the classroom, acknowledging that culturally diverse children have experiences that may not reflect the typical middle-class experiences that are part of most books and school environments. These teachers need to recognize that while their own experiences may be quite different from those of their children, nonetheless, their children's experiences are valued and their diversity is respected.

Building Background Features

7. Concepts explicitly linked to students' background experiences

---

Teachers should plan to take time during lessons to ask students what they know about a topic. Before reading a story about a girl going to her grandmother's house, ask about their experiences visiting a grandparent. Besides providing important oral language practice opportunities for the children, it piques their interest in the story when the teacher makes an explicit link by saying, "Those are interesting adventures. Well, we're going to read about a girl who visited her grandmother. Let's see if her experience is like yours." Perhaps most importantly, when children talk about their experiences, it helps the teacher get to know each child better and provides insight about them and their lives. During the lesson in Figure 4.2, the children made a Feeling Book by drawing faces that showed emotions, such as nervous or happy. The teacher could have simply pointed to the drawing, asked for the name of the emotion, and moved on. Instead, the teacher skillfully tapped into the students' own feelings and experiences. She pointed to a face on which Marco had drawn a smile and asked, "What kind of face is this?" When Marco replied that it was a happy face, she wrote the word *happy* under the face and asked, "When do you feel happy?" Marco said that he is happy when William, a classmate, shares with him. (This is valuable information to have. If Marco has a rough day, the teacher might ask William to play with him. Also, when pairing children together, she now knows that Marco and William work well together. Marco's answer also might indicate that he is sensitive to social interactions because he mentioned a relationship rather than saying he is happy when he gets a new toy.) She went on to ask about other emotions and Marco replied that he is sad "when they put gang writing on the house" and nervous "when dad gets mad at me." Another child's comment provided a teachable moment for the objective. William drew an angry face and said that he got angry when Maurice broke his robot. The teacher talked with him about how to express anger in healthy ways, as by using words instead of hitting.

As you can see, building on the students' experiences yields a number of positive outcomes.

- Since oral language development is an important part of early learning, discussion about their background provides children with a chance to practice using oral language.

- Lessons are made more relevant when children can see a link between their experience or interest and the concept of the lesson.

- It helps the teacher get to know each child as he or she shares ideas and experiences and talks about family.

- Discussions reveal children's academic knowledge and skill level. If the lesson is an introduction to a unit on transportation, asking children what they know about the topic informs the teacher about each child's level of understanding. Some children may know that transportation involves trucks, cars, and trains; others may know specific names of cars and trucks; while others may not be able to contribute much to the discussion because their knowledge about transportation is limited. The discussion provides the teacher with useful assessment information, revealing a starting point for instruction.

- Positive student–teacher relationships are developed when teachers show genuine interest in children and give them an opportunity to talk about themselves during lessons and throughout the day.

Building Background Features

8. Links explicitly made between past learning and new concepts

---

Young children are exposed to an abundance of new information, language, and skills. English learners must work harder to negotiate meaning than their native English speaking peers because they must navigate a classroom where a new language is spoken. For this reason, early childhood teachers must provide a bridge for children between past activities and new ones. There are various ways to refresh children's memories, but the process must be explicit so that they see the relationship between previous learning and new learning. For instance, the teacher shows a picture of a truck and asks questions to review past learning: *Who remembers when we talked about transportation yesterday? What kind of transportation did we talk about? What song did we sing about trucks? Do you want to sing it again? Ok, it goes. . . .*

Another way to link past learning with new concepts is to show the materials that were used previously so that the children recall prior activities and are prepared for the new lesson. A simple direction like, "Turn and talk. Tell your partner something we did yesterday" is a valuable way to help students recall a prior lesson and also practice oral language skills. The retelling process is an important academic skill as well.

Building Background Features

9. Key vocabulary emphasized (e.g., introduced, written, repeated and highlighted for students to see)

Vocabulary development is critically important to children's overall language development. To be successful in elementary school and beyond, children need to accumulate a vocabulary of thousands of words. Yet children from families who live in poverty, including English learners, have dramatically less rich experience with language in their homes than do middle-class children (Hart & Reisley, 1995; NAEYC, 2009). Therefore, it is incumbent upon schools to provide an optimal language environment for these children. According to Resnick and Snow (2009), "Every day, preschoolers and elementary students should expand their vocabularies by learning a handful of new words. This puts them on track to learn hundreds of new words every year—a reasonable expectation as they progress through school." (p. 8).

Words may be learned incidentally or taught explicitly. An example of explicit teaching took place when children worked on the Feeling Book, and words were used to label each emotion. Another example of explicit teaching would be a lesson that uses the emotion words to focus on phonological awareness, such as initial sounds (*h*appy, *n*ervous), or how phonemes change word meaning (*s*ad versus *m*ad). The emotion words were taught incidentally when the girl was looking at the Cinderella book and the vocabulary words were woven into the discussion with the teacher and assistant. Other ways that teachers can help children learn new words include the following:

- Write a caption on pictures that children draw. Ask the student to tell you what the picture represents and then write a sentence using the child's words.
- Point out new words used in conversation or in books (see example in Figure 4.4).
- Draw attention to words that have been introduced in one context and appear in another.

- Select three colors and three pieces of clothing as target vocabulary words for a week. Put these on a poster that you can use as a prop while saying, "Everyone with a red shirt can go wash your hands" (line up, etc). When the words appear in a book or song, show the children.
- Play word games with children, such as rhyming word games (e.g., ask children to change the first letter and try to make a new word so *hat* could become *cat*).
- Paraphrase for struggling speakers. For example: Student: *He goed*. Teacher: *Oh, he went to the bathroom?* Student: *Yes*.
- Add new words to posters or Word Walls, but make Word Walls that illustrate the terms as well as show the spelling. That way when a word appears in a book or conversation, you can draw students' attention to the Word Wall and the illustration will help them recall the meaning. Displaying words on a child's desk also is a good way to individualize that child's personal vocabulary goals.

As the feature description indicates, it is important to write words and post them for students to see and refer to along with their visual representation. English learners may not yet have the auditory acuity to hear all the sounds of English since some English sounds do not exist in their home language. Illustrations with words are very helpful to them because even if they can't read, per se, they begin making an association between the written and spoken word.

FIGURE 4.4

Story: Goldilocks and the Three Bears

Teacher's script:

Today we are going to read a story that I think you will like. As we read the story, I want you to notice when we come across one of our words for this week (points to the words on the board): *feeling, excited, afraid. Can you say those words with me? Feeling. Excited. Afraid. Very good. What is a feeling? We've talked about this. Remember when we made our Feelings Book? What is a feeling?* [some student responses, "like sad" etc]. *Yes, a feeling is an emotion, something we feel like sad or happy or afraid. We talked about different feelings you have. What was a feeling you had in your Feelings Book, Maurice?* [S replies]. *What about you Marisa?* [S replies]. *Everyone, turn to a partner and tell a feeling you wrote in your Feelings Book.* [students share] *Right, those are feelings. In today's story, we're going to read about a girl who has different feelings or emotions in the story. One feeling she has is that she is afraid. What does it mean to be afraid?* [S, scared]. *Right, to be scared. Show me what you look like when you're scared or afraid.* [children respond]. *Ok, what do you look like when you're excited?* [children respond].

Ok, we're going to begin reading our story and I want to you listen for those words as the story is read. What are the words again? (pointing to the board, signals for children to say along) *Feeling. Excited. Afraid. Very good. Let's be good listeners and raise your hand when you hear our words in the story. Looking at the cover, what do you think the story will be about?* [children give a variety of responses; brief discussion is followed by reading of the story]

Concluding Thoughts

As you reflect on this chapter and how the first two components of the SIOP®
Model relate to preschool classrooms, remember the following important points:

- Language, socio-emotional, physical, and cognitive development are the foundation for all activities for young learners.
- Content and language objectives guide teaching. They help the teacher focus and let children know what they are learning.
- Vocabulary development is strongly related to overall academic success. Time and attention should be given to learning new vocabulary words.
- Activities should be developed that will support successful learning experiences; this will help children develop positive attitudes toward school.

chapter 5

Using the SIOP® Model with Young Learners: Comprehensible Input and Strategies

Language and early literacy development are the primary responsibilities of early childhood education programs. In Chapter 3 we discussed language development in detail and in Chapter 4 we explored how early literacy development can be supported in the Lesson Preparation and Building Background components. In this chapter we present a lesson that capitalizes on students' interests as a way of developing early literacy skills. In many ways, language and literacy are inextricably related and cannot be separated. How do you learn anything new without thinking about it and using language for self talk? Children first learn to understand and use language orally through listening and speaking; then their understanding moves to exploring written language through reading and writing.

Throughout this book we suggest ways to develop language and early literacy in young English learners. However, the first step in interacting with your students in informal and formal learning situations is to make sure that the students understand what you are saying. Many of the comprehensible input techniques we present are essential for providing the clues needed to promote successful communication in both English and the children's home languages.

Learning is also enhanced when teachers support children's acquisition of language, concepts, information, and skills through scaffolding, by teaching children strategies for learning on their own and by using appropriate questioning techniques that check comprehension and foster higher level thinking.

Components of the SIOP® Model

In this chapter we will review the next two components, Comprehensible Input and Strategies, and discuss how the features of these components apply to young learners. In the following two chapters (Chapters 6 and 7) we will address the remaining SIOP® components.

Comprehensible Input is a component that has application across the features of the SIOP® Model because a teacher should be comprehensible to and understood by students at all times. For this to happen, teachers need to use the types of techniques we present here consistently. They are particularly valuable when communication breaks down and English learners don't understand the message the teacher is trying to convey, as is often the case with beginning speakers of English. The features of the Strategies component focus on teaching children to use learning strategies to access and remember information as well as helping teachers ask appropriate questions and support learning through scaffolding. We invite you to think about your own teaching as you read about these features.

Comprehensible Input

Comprehensible Input Features

10. Speech appropriate for students' proficiency level (e.g., slower rate, enunciation and simple sentence structure for beginners)

This feature ought to be familiar to early childhood educators; the speech behaviors listed in the feature description are typically the way language is used in ECE settings. However, it is important to keep in mind that slower speech, repetition, and enunciation are critical for English learners. In particular, using a slower rate of speech with young ELs helps them to understand the spoken message. Again, some sounds of English are likely to be new to them and some English sounds may not exist in their home language. Some letters (e.g., certain vowels) may be pronounced one way in their home language, but have multiple pronunciations in English.

Further, the average adult speaks at a rate of almost 170 words per minute, whereas the average 5- to 7-year-old processes speech at a rate of only 120 words per minute (Tobias, 2008). Imagine how much slower a 3- or 4-year-old's processing rate is since they are still learning language! Now imagine what it must be like for children whose English proficiency is lower than that of children who speak English at home. Care must be taken to speak at an appropriately slow pace with good enunciation and frequent repetition. The slower pace, however, does not mean a teacher pauses between each word. Instead, the language input must be more natural, with pauses between phrases and clauses.

The importance of listening is often overlooked in schooling, but for young English learners listening is the first language skill to develop. Most developmental charts of second language acquisition begin with a "silent" stage in which the learner is listening to the new language before attempting to speak. Listening plays a significant role in children's early literacy development and academic success (Jalongo & Li, 2010), and although development of effective listening skills merits attention, the way teachers talk to young English learners also contributes to how well they listen. Speaking in a way that is understandable to English learners is a teacher's responsibility.

Comprehensible Input Features

11. Clear explanation of academic tasks

Children learn best when they know what to do and can do it well, moving from activity to activity seamlessly. In effective preschool classrooms, activity areas are clearly marked and materials are arranged to provide visual clues about their use. For example, manipulatives are organized in bins with labels and pictures that show what they are and how they might be used; the science area has objects arranged so they are accessible for children and have cards or other visuals that show ideas for exploration. In each activity area and common space, visuals are used to indicate expectations for the areas and their routines, for instance, with pictures by the sink to delineate the steps for washing hands.

In addition to promoting learning, another advantage of making procedures and expectations clear is that it may reduce misbehavior. In our observations of classes we have found that children's off-task or inappropriate behaviors are often the result of their not understanding what the expectations are. Even during center time or play time, children may become frustrated if they aren't sure about what options they have or how to use the materials.

Besides the use of visuals, effective preschool teachers introduce activities and routines through modeling. With step-by-step oral directions, teachers make the procedures (or possibilities for exploratory play) comprehensible to the young learners. Demonstrations also allow teachers to indicate appropriate and inappropriate uses of the materials. Examples of completed projects (e.g., a clock face drawn on a paper plate with paper cut-outs representing minute and hour hands attached with a paper fastener) can also guide the children's actions.

FIGURE 5.1 *Adapted from Mardell Nash's SIOP® Language Arts Lesson*

SIOP® LESSON PLAN

Class Level: Preschool – 3-year olds
Duration: 3 days/20 minutes per day
Subject: Language Arts

Theme:	Self Awareness
Lesson Topic:	My Favorite Things
Objectives:	CO: SW write about themselves in "Book About Me". LO: SW orally express information about themselves.
Key Vocabulary:	Circle, favorite, pet.
Materials:	Camera, prewritten pages for the book (see Figure 5.2), pencils, markers, computer and projector or smartboard.
Motivation:	Introduce the concept of individuality. Children are both similar and different. Begin by using a computer program such as Starfall.com's *All About Me*. Go through the questions as a group selecting one student at a time to highlight. (The program asks a student's gender, hair type and color, face color, etc.) Option if you don't use a computer program: ask students in the group questions such as Are you a boy or girl? What color is your hair? What is your favorite food to eat? and What is your pet? You may have to explain the meaning of some of the words and elicit examples from the children.
Presentation:	Go over the content and language objectives. Say, "Today you are going to write a book about yourself. I want to know so many things about you! Let's begin by taking a picture of each of you to glue into your book." (The teacher will make a book about herself along with the children.) After taking photos of each child, say, "Let's look through the book and see what information you will tell me about yourself." Read through each of the pages that students will complete. Pause after each page and have them tell a partner what their favorite color is, what their pet is, and their favorite food is.
Practice & Application:	Say, "Now it's time to write your book. Let's begin by writing your name. Notice on the first page it says, 'My name is _____' and there is a space to write your name. Please write your name on the line. If you need to, copy the letters of your name from your name tag on your desk." Help children write their names. Accept any proximate writing including scribbles. Help the children glue the photo on the page. Let children work at their own pace on the pages. They continue completing 1-2 pages.
Review & Assessment:	At the end of the activity, review the objectives and vocabulary words. Then ask each student to "read" a page(s) they completed to the group. Scaffold the language as needed and assess student learning.
Extension:	The books can be placed in the Book Corner for later reading. The pages are self-explanatory since the child's picture is on the front, the circle is colored with his/her favorite color, and so on. These visual clues provide the meaning of the words.

FIGURE 5.2

My name is   (kid writing here) .

(CHILD'S PHOTO)

My favorite color is   (kid writing here) .

(CRAYON COLORED CIRCLE)

Comprehensible Input Features

12. A variety of techniques used to make content concepts clear (e.g., modeling, visuals, hands-on activities, demonstrations, gestures, body language)

For English learners who have limited comprehension of spoken English, the teacher uses an abundance of techniques to make the message understood. These techniques are geared to the child's proficiency level, with many more clues provided for beginning speakers. Many techniques are found in the SIOP® text for elementary teachers (Echevarria, Vogt & Short, 2010a). Some of those techniques include:

- *Use gestures, body language, and objects to accompany speech.* Use gestures to accompany words to make common classroom directions understandable, such as "Come to circle," or "sit down"; gestures can help convey the meaning of new vocabulary words. Use objects and visual cues, such as tape on the floor to indicate where to sit, shapes to show where to hang sweaters and backpacks, placemats to show where to put bowls, and so on.

- *Provide a model of a process, task, or assignment.* Use models and posters to teach common routines such as what to do with trash and/or dishes after snack, and establish rules for specific classroom areas and/or activities (e.g., circle time, housekeeping, dramatic play). Physical models and realia related to concepts like transportation can promote better student understanding. Audio models (e.g., songs on CD, books on tape) may also provide comprehensible input for the learners.

● *Preview material before introducing a lesson.* When the class gets new toys, introduce them and show their purpose. For example, with a new Legos® set say, "These are the parts" and give the names for each, saying, "This is what they can do." It is useful to also demonstrate what should not be done, such as putting items in their mouths. Put new materials in the dramatic play area (e.g., drug store) and say, "These are the names of the new pieces of equipment; here are roles that can be played." Provide specific words that can help with each such as, "I want a _____" or "Can I help you?" or "Welcome to _____."

● *Use sentence strips or a series of pictures* to review events in a story, or to put events of the story in sequential order.

● *Display graphic organizers* to depict key information, relationships among words or concepts, and so forth.

At the beginning of the lesson in Figure 5.1, we observed that one child started writing letters of his name on the bottom of the page in his book rather than as part of the sentence, "My name is_____." Teachers cannot assume children have the prerequisite skills for reading and writing such as moving from top to bottom of a page or from left to right. Showing a model of a completed book would have given the student the support he needed to be successful in writing the first page of his own book. It is not uncommon to see English learners (and other children) appear a bit lost or confused about what the expectation is. We want children to experience success in every lesson so that in these early years they develop positive attitudes about school and learning. Opportunities for success and positive experiences come about when the right amount of support is provided to the child, including modeling. (Additional types of support are found in other SIOP® features.)

Strategies

This component refers to both learning strategies that we can teach to young children so they can acquire and reflect on information themselves and instructional strategies that teachers use to help children during the classroom learning process.

Strategies Features

13. Ample opportunities provided for students to use learning strategies

---

● Research tells us that successful learners use strategies to assist in understanding, remembering, and recalling information, whereas struggling learners typically do not. Explicitly and carefully teaching children to use a variety of strategies will improve their learning. The instruction should include naming a strategy and giving the students multiple opportunities over time to practice using it. These opportunities ideally would involve different objects, genres, or settings to ensure understanding. Two types of learning strategies that are particularly applicable to young learners are cognitive strategies and social/affective strategies (Chamot & O'Malley, 2009).

- Cognitive strategies are techniques used by learners to complete a task. Examples of cognitive strategies include using manipulatives to count objects or solve math problems; referring to pictures of key concepts and vocabulary to render meaning; making connections between the story and children's experiences prior to or after story reading; using materials and activities to engage children when doing activities such as role playing or block building; playing letter games; and making comparisons. In ECE settings, strategies may be taught during both individual and group learning tasks.

- Social/affective strategies refer to the influences on learning posed by the child's interactions with others and his or her comfort with the environment. Learning is impeded if a child is stressed or feels threatened; and learning is enhanced when individuals work cooperatively to problem solve or complete a project, when they participate in a group discussion, or when they help each other to clarify something they are confused about. The teacher pays attention to children's affective cues, is intentional about setting up peer interactions to support social/affective needs, introduces appropriate vocabulary to describe feelings, and praises children's use of language to self advocate, such as when a boy pinches a girl while standing in line and the girl says, "I don't like that." The teacher responds with, "Nice job of using your words."

Strategies Features

14. Scaffolding techniques consistently used, assisting and supporting student understanding (e.g., think-alouds)

Scaffolding, or providing support to enhance students' understanding or expression, is a natural part of good instruction for young learners. As you can see in the lesson in Figure 5.1, the teacher uses two types of scaffolding: procedural and verbal (Echevarria, Vogt & Short, 2010a).

Procedural scaffolding refers to the instructional supports teachers offer to ensure a positive, successful learning outcome for children. These involve assisting and supporting children's understanding by, for instance, using predictable routines and directions during typical classroom activities, pairing inexperienced children with experienced children as peer helpers, pairing English learners with English speakers to foster English language development, including pictures to describe rules and procedures at centers, and doing a picture walk before shared reading to develop language.

In the lesson shown in Figure 5.1, a group of children is becoming more self-aware and practicing writing skills by composing a Book About Me. The book consists of 5 pages, and each page has a sentence that tells something about the child such as favorite color or favorite food. On the cover page, the children write their names. If they cannot write their names independently, the children have the option of copying from their laminated name tags. They complete the sentence:

My name is _____

English learners may need to have the sentence translated for understanding, if possible, by a teacher, paraprofessional, parent volunteer, or another student. If translation isn't possible, comprehensible input techniques are used to convey meaning. The teacher asks each child, "What is your name?" and encourages the child to answer, "My name is...." Some students will be able to answer spontaneously, whereas others will require the scaffold of repeating what the teacher says. The teacher uses a camera to take each child's picture and they glue it on the front page. The next page of the book says, "My favorite color is _____." There is a circle for the children to color in with their favorite color. Children are invited to be creative and to design the page as they like. Again, when possible, the teacher translates and assists those students who need support. Other supports for children who need them include having the teacher or paraprofessional write a word for the student to model writing if he or she is not yet ready to write the word independently.

Further, instruction is scaffolded for individual learning objectives. Teaching is modified to support the specified needs of each child, based on assessment information. In the example above, let's say a child has difficulty holding a pencil and a goal for her is to work on fine motor skills. During the Book About Me activity, the teacher might write the word the child dictates in highlighter pen and the child traces on top of the word. Or, the teacher might provide support by assisting her in holding the pencil and writing her own words. Another idea is for the child to simply draw as a way of practicing fine motor skills.

Verbal scaffolding is used to support beginning speakers and also to assist more proficient English learners in reaching higher levels of English proficiency. Teachers take students at their current level and use prompting, questioning, paraphrasing, and elaboration to improve their English language development. An example of verbal scaffolding with a beginning English speaker is seen in the following teacher–student exchange. A student began working on a page with a circle to color with the caption, "My favorite color is_____."

T: "What is your favorite color?"

S: "Green"

T: "Green? Oh, I like green, too. Can you color this shape green? What is this shape?" [points to a circle]

S: [silence]

T: "Can you tell me the name of this shape?" [points to a circle] "What it is in Spanish?"

S: [silence]

T: "Do you know the name in Spanish?"

S: "Círculo."

. . . . Components of the SIOP® ●

53

T: "That's right, círculo. And in English it sounds almost the same. Circle. This is a circle." [points to the circle] "What is it in Spanish?"

S: "Círculo."

T: "Excellent, and what is it in English?"

S: "Circle."

T: "That's right. Now can you color the circle green?"

S: [nods and begins coloring]

In this way, the teacher provided some of the language the student didn't have. She encouraged the student to produce language without pressuring him, and she guided him to use a word that had been introduced but that he had not yet acquired (circle). She also made an explicit link to the child's home language, which is another way of scaffolding: building on what is known and extending that knowledge to new learning.

Verbal scaffolding assists and supports children's understanding through interacting and encouraging language use such as repeating or restating what the child said with standard English usage; engaging in nondirective conversation, focusing children's attention on specific language features; and using repetition to demonstrate correct pronunciation. Also, a think-aloud is an effective and easily used scaffold. In a lesson we observed in Tina Easter's Head Start class, she articulated her thoughts this way: "First I'll get some beans, then I'll count them, 1, 2, 3, 4, 5—I have 5 beans. Teresa, how many beans do you have? (count together, 1 to 3) Okay, you have 3. Who has more? Let's see. I'll take away two from my group and two from yours. Let's take one more from each. Okay, yours are gone, but I still have two beans. So I had more. Let's do another one. Who has more, Jose or Mariko?" If students cannot answer the question, the teacher again scaffolds with a Think-aloud: "Let's see. Mariko has 1, 2, 3—3 beans and Jose has 1, 2, 3, 4—4 beans. Who has more? I think Jose has more because he has 4 beans and Mariko has 3, right?"

In kindergarten, the teacher might ask about counting to 10. She counts out 7 beans, and then asks the students: "How many more beans do I need to get to 10? Let me use my counting line and see. My finger is at 7 and I will count on. 8, 9, 10. That's three more." The counting line is an instructional scaffold for the students as they learn to count, add, and subtract on their own.

Scaffolding is used whenever students need support in learning situations and it can be provided in the form of verbal scaffolding or procedural scaffolding.

Strategies Features

15. A variety of question types used including those that promote higher-order thinking skills (e.g., open-ended questions rather than questions with yes/no responses)

In settings with young children, we want talk, talk, and more talk. One way to encourage child talk is by asking questions. Questioning serves a number of purposes.

- *Developing language.* Asking children open-ended questions that will elicit talk about their experiences or ideas provides an opportunity to practice oral language and use new vocabulary.

- *Engaging children's thinking.* We want children to think about what they are doing and what they will do next. Planning is a valuable academic skill. To encourage clarification about a procedure, for example, ask: "What comes next?" Children's thinking is stimulated as they think through the process.

- *Modeling how to ask questions.* Children need to learn such skills as how to ask for help and how to seek information. When the teacher models asking appropriate questions, children are learning this important skill and language function. When they converse in pairs, such as in a role play between a buyer and a store clerk, they can practice asking and answering questions.

- *Recalling information or events.* Questioning is an effective way to review previous learning and engage children's recall. For example, "Who can tell us what we learned about sharks?" Children give a few replies and the teacher says, "Can you tell me more about that? Where did it live? What color was it?"

Teachers use these questions in informal conversations and while teaching lessons—any time there is an opportunity to stimulate language use. We offer one piece of advice, however. When students respond to a question with only one or two words, try to encourage more extended replies from them with prompts such as "Can you tell me more?" and "What do you mean by that?"

Concluding Thoughts

As you reflect on this chapter and how these two components of the SIOP® Model are used in preschool classrooms, remember the following important points:

- Language needs to be comprehensible to children.
- Learning is influenced by how students perceive the environment and how well they use strategies to organize, remember, and recall information.
- Teachers assist student learning through scaffolding, by providing the amount of support each child needs to be successful and moving the child step by step to independent work.

chapter 6

Using the SIOP® Model with Young Learners: Interaction and Practice & Application

The components of the SIOP® Model discussed in this chapter are of particular importance to young learners because of the extensive language development that takes place during the early years. As discussed in detail in Chapter 2, language is the foundation for literacy. It is also the vehicle for intellectual development. Language is a tool that enables children to learn about themselves, their family and culture, and the world around them. We want children to be active learners, so it is critical that they be given the opportunity in school for talk, talk, and more talk.

Throughout this chapter we will refer to the math lesson found in Figure 6.1. This lesson is designed to be taught with lots of interaction and discussion as students practice and apply the concept of putting items in order by size. Some teachers may be tempted to use the lesson plan for a teacher-dominated lesson in which the teacher

FIGURE 6.1 *Adapted from Charlotte Daniel's SIOP® Math Lesson Plan*

SIOP® LESSON PLAN

Class Level: Pre-K
Class Periods: 5 days/45 minutes Lab time
Subject: Learning Labs
Staff: Teacher, paraprofessional

Topic:	Math—Ordering by size
Content Objective:	• We will put items in order according to size.
Language Objectives:	• We will tell our teacher our prediction for how to arrange items by size. • We will listen to a classmate tell us how they put the raindrops in order. • We will use the words *bigger* and *smaller*. This raindrop is _____ than this raindrop.
Key Vocabulary:	smaller, bigger, than, raindrop, same, different, put in order, arrange
Materials:	raindrop-shaped cutouts in 6 different sizes, objects or toys of varying sizes

SIOP® Features:

Preparation	Scaffolding	Grouping Options
__ Adaptation of content	**X** Modeling	__ Whole class
X Links to background	**X** Guided practice	**X** Small groups
__ Links to past learning	__ Independent practice	**X** Partners
__ Strategies incorporated	**X** Comprehensible input	__ Independent

Integration of Processes	Application	Assessment
__ Reading	**X** Hands-on	**X** Individual
__ Writing	__ Meaningful	__ Group
X Speaking	**X** Linked to objectives	__ Written
X Listening	__ Promotes engagement	**X** Oral

Building Background:	Whole class: Show 4 toys and hold up the smallest one. Model how to arrange the items from smallest to largest. Then, divide the class into 4 groups and give each student an object or toy that varies in size from the others (e.g., a doll, a crayon and a marker). Tell students to get in line in their groups, arranged from the biggest to the smallest item. After they rearrange themselves, have them explain to each other using the sentence frames: "I'm in the right place because my toy is smaller than ___(child name)___." Or "I'm in the right place because my toy is bigger than _____(child name)____." Small group: Is everything the same size? After the students respond, agree with their response and remind them of the line that they created in order from biggest to smallest. Hold up two objects, and then ask, "Which is bigger?" "Which is smaller?" "How do you know that it is bigger/smaller?" Tell students that we are going to compare raindrops and put them in order according to size.
Presentation:	Ask a small group of children what they think they can do with a group of raindrop cutouts. Model various ways to group the raindrop cutouts. Model the language, explicitly drawing attention to the words *bigger*, *smaller* and *than* in reference to the raindrop cutouts.

(continued)

FIGURE 6.1 *Adapted from Charlotte Daniel's SIOP® Math Lesson Plan* (continued)

Practice & Application:	Students will take turns arranging the raindrop cutouts and then telling a partner which is bigger and which is smaller. The language can be elaborated to describe why the raindrop cutouts were put in that particular order. For additional practice, partners can go to a learning center and get 2 items, one bigger than the other. The partners tell which is bigger and which is smaller. Then they can compare their items to the items another pair of children retrieves.
Review & Assessment:	As children are working in partners, circulate among the pairs and make notes about individual child performance. How are they expressing themselves? Do they understand the concept? Do they use the key words?
	At the conclusion of the lesson, go over the content and language objectives and the key vocabulary. Talk about when the key words were used in the lesson. Provide a final review of objects comparing smaller and bigger. Assess learning.

does most of the talking. In SIOP® classes, the teacher is more of a facilitator, and children's exploration of language and concepts is encouraged. The teacher skillfully guides interaction, but does not get in the way of children experimenting with language (their home language and English) and figuring out new concepts and information.

Components of the SIOP® Model

In this chapter we will review the two components, Interaction and Practice & Application, and then discuss how the features of these components apply to young learners. Both the Interaction and the Practice & Application components focus on productive oral language practice and provide structured opportunities for language development. You may want to refer to Chapter 3 for a more detailed discussion of language development, including the home language, before reading this chapter.

Interaction

In some cases, the teacher is the first important English interlocutor for the youngsters in early childhood classes. Conversations between teacher and students offer repeated occasions for the teacher to model academic English and for the students to practice the language knowledge they are acquiring over time. Children in SIOP® classes are encouraged to practice oral language in every way possible and in doing so, teachers accept a variety of forms children produce including "errors." Understanding that language learning is a process, teachers do not directly correct utterances. (Providing feedback is discussed in Chapter 7.)

Interaction Features

16. Frequent opportunities for interaction and discussion between teacher/student and among students, which encourage elaborated responses about lesson concepts

---

To support oral language practice, children are provided the opportunity to experience different types of interaction with adults and peers, so they learn to use language appropriately in different contexts. (See the discussion of register in Chapter 3.) Some interaction experiences are cooperative group activities; others are peer-oriented activities. During the lesson in Figure 6.1, the teacher introduces the concept of size order to the whole group by arranging items from smaller to bigger. When the teacher shows the toys and asks which is smaller and which is bigger, she elicits a lot of language from the children. She might ask a child to select the smaller one and a bigger one as a way to engage students in interaction. Then she has students stand in small groups and gives each child a toy that varies in size from the other toys handed out. The children figure out who has the smallest toy, the next smallest, and the biggest. They line up by standing in the order of the size of their toy. The teacher and paraprofessional oversee the process, assisting as needed, but the children work together to complete the task. Once they are in order, each child uses the sentence frame, "I'm in the right place because my toy is smaller than _(Maria's)_." Or "I'm in the right place because my toy is bigger than _(Rafael's)_." In the small group activity, children interact with one another and the teacher and/or paraprofessional. As you can see, there are many opportunities for interaction throughout the lesson.

Children may interact with one another and the teacher in an endless variety of ways including:

- *Verbal games*—children love games, and verbal games develop language and literacy skills. Imitation games involve children repeating what the teacher or puppet says. Other games may involve phonemic awareness; one example is a name game in which a consonant is chosen and is used to replace the first letter of the children's names. For example, if the letter chosen for the game is R, then a child's name is picked (e.g., Cynthia). The group says a rhyme such as, "Take the C from Cynthia, cover it like so. [The teacher puts a letter R over the C from Cynthia's name tag.] Cynthia becomes Rynthia and no one else will know." Then ask the next child, "What does your name begin with?" and the first letter of the child's name is replaced with R. The game continues with other children's names.

- *Songs*—Songs for young children are simple and repetitive, which helps them to learn the words' meaning and pronunciation. Using gestures, motion, and clapping to accompany the words makes the meaning understandable and allows all children to participate even if they don't know each word. Many songs are available in multiple languages, so, for example, a greeting song may be sung first in English, and then in Spanish.

- *Rhymes and poems*—Early literacy skills get a boost when children are aware of the way that letters, sounds, and words can be manipulated and used in different ways. Rhymes and poems help children discover, for instance, that changing one letter can change the meaning of a word: from *dog* to *log* to *hog*. Alliteration can be used to show phonological patterns such as a *happy horse hopped hurriedly home.* When children memorize rhymes and poems, the words become part of their increasing vocabularies.

- *Read alouds*—A group of children are encouraged to follow along as the teacher reads a story or text. Big books and other picture books (either fiction or non-fiction) are ideal for this activity. A picture walk can preview some vocabulary for the children. Then, while reading, the teacher makes sure all children have the opportunity to talk about the story, predict what they think might happen next, tell about something similar that they have experienced, and so forth. The idea is to expose children to reading while at the same time provide maximum opportunity to interact with their peers and the teachers. Bilingual teachers are able to pepper the discussion with questions in a child's home language. For teachers who are not bilingual, when some students want to use their home language to make a point, another student may interpret for them. This practice should be encouraged so that all children can participate.

- *Peer Assisted Learning* (K-PALS) —For kindergarten students, peer-to-peer learning strategies have been shown to enhance pre-reading skills such as being able to identify letters, sounds, and ends of words, and being able to comprehend a story when it is told to them (Fuchs & Fuchs, 1998).

Be mindful that although providing opportunities for interaction is strongly encouraged, English learners should not be put on the spot to participate if they are not ready or are uncomfortable. Initially accept whatever level of participation they wish. Some English learners, especially older preschoolers and kindergarteners, may be more comfortable using English in front of peers when they have a prop such as a puppet or an animal that they pretend is doing the talking. It may take the pressure off the child who thinks he must use English correctly in front of peers. However, all children should be encouraged to participate rather than the teacher calling on only those who volunteer to talk. Some ways to get students involved are to randomly select names from a pocket chart or from a can with tongue depressor sticks that have each child's name written on one.

Interaction Features

17. Grouping configurations support language and content objectives of the lesson

---

In order for children to interact with one another and with the teacher in meaningful ways, attention needs to be given to the way groups are organized. Children should take part in a variety of grouping patterns such as large group, small groups, and partners, as well as individual learning situations. Effective classroom grouping patterns find children sitting together in self-selected groups or alone on the floor or in activity areas; playing with a partner; working in a small group; and sitting together on the rug as a whole group. The type of grouping depends on the nature of the activity and whether it is a teacher-directed or child-directed activity. In the math lesson in Figure 6.1, whole class grouping was best for introducing the concept, but small groups allowed for more focused exploration as students worked in partners.

Having a variety of groups promotes interaction. A teacher can interact more personally with an individual child or a small group, but a whole group setting is ideal for activities that generate more energy such as singing, role-playing, dancing, and so forth. Also, variety allows children to participate in settings that are most comfortable for them. Some children enjoy working with a partner, whereas others prefer a larger group.

Finally, children learning English benefit from being paired with English speakers so that they have an English language model and a partner who understands the language of the teacher and can assist in their participation in learning activities. Also, when an English learner is grouped with others who are bilingual, they interpret and assist in participation as well.

Interaction Features

18. Sufficient wait time for student response consistently provided

---

Young children are hearing new words used every day, and it takes time for them to process language. This is even more applicable for English learners. They need to process the question or statement—and perhaps translate it in their heads—then formulate a response mentally in English and say it in English. Teachers need to provide children with time to go through this procedure and then wait patiently for a response. They may count to five silently before asking for a response from the child.

Further, in many U.S. schools, the pace of speaking is quite fast, and speakers are typically uncomfortable with a lot of time or pauses between utterances. For example, when teachers ask questions in class, if someone doesn't volunteer a response immediately, the teacher usually calls on someone to speak or answers the question herself. A lengthy lag in the discussion isn't typical for our speech patterns. However, wait time varies by culture. In some cultures, it is common to have a pause between utterances, and individuals are comfortable with periods of silence. In other cultures, more than one person may speak at the same time with little or no wait time. When teaching English learners, wait time is necessary to allow for processing language. Young students with disabilities also benefit from wait time since they may have auditory processing difficulties.

Interaction Features

19. Ample opportunities for students to clarify key concepts in L1 as needed with aide, peer, or L1 text

---

It is especially critical for young English learners to use their home language as they are acquiring a second language so that they are able to express themselves and understand others in the language used by their family. First language development has social and cognitive benefits, and students should use their home language freely in school. Studies have shown that the home language is lost at an alarming rate during the first years of schooling, particularly when children aren't provided an opportunity to practice using it (Bernhard & Pacini-Ketchabaw, 2010). Please refer to Chapter 3 for a more thorough discussion of the issue of first language development.

Whenever possible, children are given the opportunity to have concepts, vocabulary, routines, activities, and so forth explained in their home language. In one class we observed, a child had worked alone at the art center. When he was finished, he left without putting everything away. The teacher took him back and told him that the scissors went in the can and the paper went in the bin. She walked away and he followed her. She took him back again and explained it again, but he walked away afterward. Finally, she gave him the instruction in Khmer, his home language, and sure enough, he put everything away!

In the lesson in Figure 6.1, the paraprofessional translated concepts and vocabulary for children as needed. Also in their partner work, children sometimes used their home language to tell which raindrop was smaller or bigger or to explain how they arranged the raindrops in groups. The point of the lesson is to understand the concept that objects may be put in order according to size. It doesn't matter which language children express their knowledge in as long as they learn the lesson's concept. After the students understand the concept, the teacher can then focus on English vocabulary and phrases that articulate the concept.

Practice & Application

The features of this component are implemented well when the teacher plans specific opportunities for children to practice using material they have learned and applying it in new ways.

Practice & Application Features

20. Hands-on materials and/or manipulatives provided for students to practice using new content knowledge

---

As mentioned previously, early childhood programs have a variety of materials for children to use that facilitate hands-on experiences. The key is to use the materials in a way that promotes the learning objectives and provides practice with new concepts and learning English. Included in these materials should be a variety of writing tools and examples of writing in English and the home languages, plenty of picture stories, and models of objects. Puppets, action figures, stuffed animals, and the like can be used in role-plays and simulations in which students practice their oral communication skills.

Children from language minority and low income households may not have had practice with pre-academic experiences that preschoolers from English speaking or middle class households have had prior to formal schooling. They may not have named animals at the zoo, visited a museum and talked about the displays, or looked for books in the library. Thus, it is important to expose English learners to picture books and objects that represent these experiences so that they can practice

● ·

62

and apply concepts associated with these topics, which they will encounter as part of academic instruction.

In sum, this feature reminds teachers to use appropriate and effective learning materials that help children be actively engaged in learning and language development.

Practice & Application Features

21. Activities provided for students to apply content and language knowledge in the classroom

---

Once a skill or new knowledge has been introduced, there needs to be ample opportunity to apply the skill or concept through classroom activities. For example, in a class of Spanish-speaking children, the concept for the week is identifying rhyming words. This is an important concept for early reading, so that children recognize the similar final sounds among rhyming words. The teacher introduces the concept by reading a short story that has a pattern of rhyming words. As she points out and repeats several pairs of rhyming words, the teacher asks if students noticed anything about the words. Then the teacher gives an example of rhyming words in Spanish, e.g., *oso/poso, pato/gato.* The children are then paired up by proficiency level, with an English speaker paired with an English learner. Each pair has picture cards with rhyming words, e.g., *cat/bat, ball/hall.* One child says the word that corresponds to the picture card and then the partner says the word on the other picture card. The teacher and paraprofessional closely supervise and scaffold for the children who need it. After the children have said rhyming words several times with their partner, the teacher shuffles the cards and redistributes them to the children. The children then mingle with one another, saying the word on their picture card and trying to find a person with the corresponding rhyming word. The teacher and paraprofessional assist as needed.

In this way, students aren't simply listening to the teacher tell about rhyming words, but instead, they have an opportunity to practice and apply the concept themselves. Particularly with young learners, teacher talk that involves instruction should be minimal; a small chunk of information should be followed by lots of student talking and doing.

For a kindergarten example of practice and application of a concept, please see Chapter 8, Figure 8.4.

Practice & Application Features

22. Activities integrate all language skills (i.e., reading, writing, listening, and speaking)

The features of the SIOP® Model are interrelated rather than independent parts of a lesson. As children participate in practice and application activities that integrate reading, writing, speaking, and listening, multiple SIOP® features are also evident. Features such as building on student background experiences, scaffolding, and highlighting vocabulary are woven into the activity.

The value of integrating all four language skills has been shown in several research studies with young ELs. In one project, the goal was to promote early biliteracy with 3- to 5-year-old children by having families, educators (family child care providers and center-based care providers), and the children create bilingual books. The topics of these books were family histories, the children's lives, and the children's interests. Photographs and children's drawings were used to illustrate the books. The books were laminated and used in both the classroom and at home for repeated reading. Students who participated in the program showed greater gains in language and literacy development than students who didn't participate (described in Bernhard & Pacini-Ketchabaw, 2010).

Integration of language skills is equally valuable as children get older. In a project with at-risk 8-year-old English learners who were from low socioeconomic homes, teachers asked students to write about their own experiences and then modeled for them how to improve their writing by adding descriptive language, dialogue, and more detail. Students who participated in the project scored significantly higher on the state assessment in writing than did students who were not part of the project (described in Echevarria & Vogt, 2010).

In both of these situations, English learners were provided with the opportunity to talk about what they knew and what was of interest to them, to put their ideas in writing, to observe models of good writing, to receive feedback on their writing, and to read the completed versions. Many of the features of the SIOP® Model were integrated in the process, and the project gave students a chance to practice and apply literacy skills.

Other child-generated texts and stories involve children dictating to their teachers. These texts and stories are meaningful to children because they reflect their own experiences, interests, and family and community relationships. For example, after finishing the lesson in Figure 6.1, the teacher may ask children to tell him what they know about a topic such as ordering from smaller to bigger. The teacher writes a summary of the children's dictation, which may be in English or the child's home language. Another way to generate text is for children to illustrate an experience or lesson concept and then tell what they have illustrated to the teacher, who writes the words as a caption. Over time, children often move from using the home language to English in their dictation and "read" the information, texts, or captions to their parents, interpreting it for them if necessary. This practice of involving parents is hoped to be the beginning of a lifelong dialogue between parent and child about school and learning.

Informational text has recently become of greater importance in elementary and secondary schools, so when children begin their early literacy experiences by dictating information as a way of creating books, it may better prepare them for later schooling experiences.

Concluding Thoughts

As you reflect on this chapter and how the first six components of the SIOP® Model apply to preschool classrooms, remember the following important points:

- Oral language development is highly correlated with reading ability. Providing opportunities for children to interact with one another and adults builds oral language skills.
- The development of bilingual skills (English and the home language) has cognitive, linguistic, and social benefits and should be encouraged in preschool and kindergarten classrooms during this critical period of language and literacy development.
- Children benefit from opportunities to practice and apply the concepts, information, and skills they have learned in meaningful ways that involve reading, writing, listening, and speaking.

Using the SIOP® Model with Young Learners: Lesson Delivery and Review & Assessment

As mentioned previously, the features of the SIOP® Model are not independent of one another, even though we are explaining each one individually. They work most effectively when they are integrated consistently in learning activities. The components in this chapter focus on how well the lesson, or learning activity, is delivered. Naturally, the execution of the lesson relates to its preparation and the teacher's skill with managing the students. As they work through the lesson, SIOP® teachers also conduct ongoing and frequent assessments of children's English language acquisition and their development in different domains. This can be done as students interact with one another and the teacher, and as children practice and apply concepts and skills. On occasion, there may be more formalized assessments of student progress as well.

Components of the SIOP® Model

In this chapter we will review the final two SIOP® components: Lesson Delivery and Review & Assessment. As we go through the features of these components, we will refer to the science lesson in Figure 7.1. The theme of the unit is Earth Day, and this particular lesson is about water pollution. As you will see, the learning activity builds both language and concept development around the topic of pollution.

Lesson Delivery

The features of Lesson Delivery are closely related to Lesson Preparation (Chapter 4) because they reflect how well the lesson, or learning activity, supports the objectives. This component also considers the extent to which children are engaged and how well the lesson is paced for the developmental levels of the children. As you read through this component, you might want to refer back to the discussion of objectives in Chapter 4.

Lesson Delivery Features

23. Content objectives clearly supported by lesson delivery
24. Language objectives clearly supported by lesson delivery

As we discuss in detail in Chapter 4, language and content objectives are modified for young learners. In preschool in particular, and to an extent in kindergarten, instruction takes multiple forms, such as directed play, spontaneous teaching moments, and teacher-directed learning opportunities. As such, the teacher takes the opportunity to skillfully weave the objectives into the activities. The science lesson example found in Figure 7.1 is quite focused on specific objectives that students will achieve during the learning activity. At other times during the day, these objectives might be reinforced in a less straightforward way. For example, a sensory activity during center time might let the children explore the sensation of shaving cream sprayed on a table. As the children play with the shaving cream, choosing to rub it around on the table, draw pictures in it, rub it on their hands, and so forth, the teacher would talk about how clean it smells. Toward the end of the time, she might pour some dirty water on one small area of the table and ask what happened to the shaving cream. Children would see that it became dirty. In this way, the teacher doesn't disrupt the children's individual exploration, but indirectly reinforces one of the objectives of the lesson: to talk about opposites related to pollution such as *clean* and *dirty*.

Content and language objectives are supported in the classroom in a number of ways:

- The teacher orally states objectives and draws attention to their visual display. (See examples in Chapter 4, Figure 4.1 and Figure 7.2 and the discussion in Chapter 8 about how teachers at one school, Roundy Elementary, use colors to distinguish content and language objectives.)

FIGURE 7.1 *Adapted from Charlotte Daniel's SIOP® Science Lesson Plan*

SIOP® LESSON PLAN

Class Level: Pre-K
Class Periods: 3 days/half-hour
Subject: Science

Topic:	Water Pollution—Earth Day Theme
Content Objective:	• We will identify causes of water pollution. • We will compare clean and dirty water
Language Objectives:	• We will answer questions and orally tell what happens when we mix oil with water. • We will use words that are opposites to talk about water pollution.
Key Vocabulary:	mix, won't mix, clean, dirty, safe, unsafe, pollution
Materials:	2-liter bottle, water, cooking oil, visual examples of water pollution, smaller clear plastic bottles with the labels taken off, one for each group of 3-4 students, a drink of water in a clear plastic glass (one for each student), chart paper for a KWL.

SIOP® Features:

Preparation
__ Adaptation of content
✗ Links to background
__ Links to past learning
__ Strategies incorporated

Scaffolding
__ Modeling
__ Guided practice
__ Independent practice
✗ Comprehensible input

Grouping Options
✗ Whole class
__ Small groups
✗ Partners
__ Independent

Integration of Processes
✗ Reading
__ Writing
✗ Speaking
✗ Listening

Application
✗ Hands-on
__ Meaningful
__ Linked to objectives
__ Promotes engagement

Assessment
✗ Individual
__ Group
__ Written
✗ Oral

Building Background:	Show a picture of dirty water and a clean swimming pool. Compare the dirty water to water in a pool. Talk about what the children see. Where would they want to swim? Why? Which place looks cleaner? Ask the students if they know the word *pollution*. What does it mean? Ask if they have seen dirty water in a local river, lake, ocean (depending on what bodies of water are nearby). Show pictures of the polluted Gulf Coast. Ask them what they remind them of. Show pictures of a pool again or a clear lake. Ask: Which one is clean? Which one is dirty? How do we know the water is clean? Give each student a clear plastic glass of water to drink.
Presentation	Tell students that we are going to make a mini ocean. State that in some places, oceans are clean and sometimes the oceans are dirty or polluted. Question the students to find out what they already know about pollution by starting a KWL chart and recording their ideas under K (What do we know?). Review lesson objectives with the class. See Figure 7.2 for a child-friendly version.
Practice & Application:	Whole group: Demonstrate adding oil to the bottle of water. Allow several students to shake the bottle, attempting to get the oil and water to mix. **Teacher: What happens when we mix water and oil?** **Student: When we mix water and oil, the _____ (or the student just answers the question without the stem according to language development level.)**

(continued)

FIGURE 7.1 *Adapted from Charlotte Daniel's SIOP(R) Science Lesson Plan (continued)*

Practice & Application *(continued)*:	On the KWL chart, add "oil and water do not mix" under **K**.
	Give each small group of 3-4 children a small clear plastic bottle containing water and oil. They can each shake it themselves and see what happens. Ask the groups what happened when oil and water were mixed. Build on their language responses. Complete the worksheet together (Figure 7.3)
	Bring the whole group back together. The big question here is: "Would you want to drink the water in the bottle? It looks clear. But we know there is oil in it." The point is that sometimes water is polluted. That is why scientists check the water that we drink and make sure it is clean. We don't want to drink water that is dirty. Ask the students: "Why don't we drink dirty water?" Accept their answers and if necessary, clarify: "Because it can make us sick."
Review & Assessment:	Whole group: Review what happened with each of the bottles. Review the key vocabulary. Check individually while in the small groups to see if each student can use the sentence, "Oil and water do not mix."
	Keep the bottles in a learning center for further review.

FIGURE 7.2

Content Objectives
Water pollution

Clean water

Language Objectives
Oil and water together

FIGURE 7.3

Read and Draw

What happens when we mix oil and water?

Water   Oil

- The teacher tells children the purpose of center or learning activities and points out pictures that show routines and explains how objects are used.
- The teacher models new activities or routines for the students.
- Learning areas are labeled in English as well as children's home languages.
- The teacher provides a reminder about participation rules.

During lesson delivery, the teacher explicitly states the activity's content and language objectives and refers back to them as the lesson plays out. Recall that since much of what is learned in the early years is language based, we suggest you not worry too much about distinguishing between content and language objectives, especially for a literacy-related learning activity. Still, it is important to maintain the routine of having both types posted so children are aware of the importance of language and expect both objectives in preschool lessons and beyond. The teacher tells students the words they will learn and use during lessons and provides opportunities to practice and apply new vocabulary words. (See Chapter 6 for more on Practice & Application.)

A review of the science lesson (Figure 7.1) shows that there are a number of specific content and language objectives stated. You may choose to have fewer, depending on the age and developmental level of your students and on the length of the activity.

Lesson Delivery Features

25. Students engaged approximately 90–100% of the period

At first glance, this feature may seem impossible to use with young children who have short attention spans and wiggly bodies! However, the intent of the features is tied to lesson planning. We don't mean that the children need to be talking all the time, but they should be on task and productive whether the task is play or academically oriented. Teachers achieve this by making sure that activities are well planned and well thought out so that children are happily occupied throughout the activity period. This is best accomplished when children

- Are on task because work areas are well marked and the routines are clear.
- Are actively involved in meaningful, interesting learning opportunities using a variety of engaging materials.
- Have enough supplies for each individual to participate fully.
- Are paying attention because they understand what the teacher is saying through use of Comprehensible Input techniques (see Chapter 5) and/or use of their home language.

Lesson Delivery Features

26. Pacing of the lesson appropriate to the students' ability level

---

For young children, learning activities are paced at a rate appropriate to their developmental levels. For kindergarteners, a typical period of instruction would not be more than 30 minutes. For preschoolers, it would be less. Teachers need to pay attention to the pace at which information is provided to young learners and to check frequently to make sure they understand (see the next section on Review & Assessment). English learners in particular may struggle when a lot of information is thrust upon them in a language they do not yet understand completely. Visual clues can only go so far when the amount of information is overwhelming. In the science lesson (Figure 7.1), the pace of the information presented would be adjusted to the age and developmental levels of the children. Perhaps this lesson would take place over 5 days for younger children rather than the 3 that are suggested on the lesson plan.

Further, the rate of speech can be difficult for children to understand. Research indicates that there is a gap between what a child hears and what he or she understands because adults speak too fast for children's level of language development. The result of this gap in understanding can sometimes be interpreted as inattention, confusion, or defiance on the part of the young learners when actually teachers need to slow their speech (Tobias, 2008).

Review & Assessment

As we mentioned earlier, although this final component is the last one in the written structure of the SIOP® Model, review and assessment take place throughout a lesson. A lesson may begin with a review of previous material or with an assessment of what the children know about a topic. Also, we heartily encourage checking comprehension and providing feedback to students on their language output and task progress throughout a lesson. The features of review and assessment also pay particular attention to review of vocabulary, given the importance of word knowledge on school success, and to review of content concepts, so students have foundational knowledge upon which to base new learning.

Review & Assessment Features

27. Comprehensive review of key vocabulary

Vocabulary development is considered the cornerstone of reading acquisition (Wasik, 2010). In Chapter 3, we discussed the importance of vocabulary development. It is estimated that by age 3, children in professional families have heard 30 million words, children in working-class families have heard 20 million words, and children in families receiving welfare have heard 10 million (Hart & Risley, 1995). In order for children to learn new words well enough to internalize them and make them part of their vocabulary, they must have repeated exposure to and practice with the words in a variety of contexts. For each lesson, the teacher selects several words that are important for understanding the content of the lesson and the classroom routines being presented. These are the key vocabulary words. Throughout a lesson, effective preschool teachers point out these key words in books read aloud and in conversation. Key words are written for students to see and review for a given learning activity. The key words in the science lesson include *mix, won't mix, clean, dirty, safe, unsafe, pollution*. It is unlikely that most pre-K English learners would learn all these words incidentally. The role of the teacher is critical in providing children with focused attention on vocabulary learning.

Review & Assessment Features

28. Comprehensive review of key content concepts

With young children, concepts need to be revisited multiple times in various ways throughout the day or across several days. In the science lesson, students learned that when water gets dirty, or polluted, it isn't safe to drink. We already mentioned a way that the concept could be reviewed during the sensory activity with shaving cream. Reading a book about water pollution or watching a video about water pollution are other ways to review the concept. Teachers can also use flannel board stories or puppets to talk about water pollution, as well as art, writing activities, and songs that are linked to the concept.

Games also can be used for review. For example, the teacher can create puzzles by taking magazine pictures of clean and dirty water, backing them with cardstock, and cutting them into pieces. Each puzzle is placed in a baggie and put in a learning center. Children find baggies with puzzle pieces and work together to assemble them. When they are finished, the teacher asks questions about the puzzles to elicit key vocabulary and encourage oral language practice.

As the teacher works with or observes the children interfacing with the concept throughout the day, she can assess their learning. In addition, she can take advantage of "teachable" moments by reviewing concepts and reinforcing vocabulary within the context of ongoing classroom activities. For example, when children are playing outside, she may discuss that the water left in puddles after a rain is "dirty." She might help students "mix" ingredients during a snack preparation activity and emphasize the need to keep cooking utensils "clean."

Review & Assessment Features

29. Regular feedback provided to students on their output (e.g., language, content, work)

Teachers' encouragement of the students in their classes is a vitally important component in the youngsters' development of positive attitudes about themselves as learners and establishment of a positive relationship with school and school personnel. We want to create situations where students can be successful and feel comfortable experimenting with language and participating in learning situations. We want children to take chances in a nonthreatening environment. Therefore, feedback must be given sensitively and kindly. When providing feedback, be encouraging:

- T: "Robert, pull up another chair, the blue chair." [S goes toward green stool.] T: "The blue chair." [S goes toward blue chair.] T: "There you go!"
- T: "Show me the fish." [S holds up a bird card.] T: "Try again." [S holds up a cat card.] T: "Try again, buddy." [S holds up a fish card.]. T: "Awesome. That is a fish."
- T: "I know you can do a great job of helping me by cleaning up over there. Thank you."

Speak calmly and clearly: Children respond to the tone set by adults. If you speak harshly or scold children, they will respond to one another in the same way, creating behavior issues. Set a calm, positive tone. Use words that they know.

- When a student gets upset or frustrated, say gently: "Take a deep breath. Have a calm body." It is especially helpful if you can demonstrate the activity to provide a model for the child to follow.
- When children run indoors, say, "Walking feet, my friends."
- When there is a conflict between children, say, "Be a peacemaker," and hold up your hand.
- When students don't know how to express themselves, provide a language model. This teaches children how to use language appropriately in different contexts.
- When a child pushes another student who is sitting next to him, say, "Say, 'Sit up please.' Don't push when he leans on you. Use your words."
- When a child is passing out items and skips someone, say, "What can you say to let him know you need one? Say, 'May I have one please?'"

Catch students doing something right. Feedback can shape behavior when attention is given to children doing the right thing rather than pointing out who is doing the wrong thing.

- "I like what you did. You pushed your chair under the table."
- "Fernando, I like the way you said, 'Excuse me please.'"
- When a child shares with another who was complaining, say, "You've been a peacemaker all day. Thank you."

Teach them to self-correct; rather than pointing out what errors children made on the task, see if they can discover it on their own.

- Show them the model of a completed product and ask how theirs looks different.
- Have them partner with another child who has the skill developed so they can work together to figure out where errors occurred.
- Ask children where they can see errors in their work or, with behavior, ask what they might have done differently.

Providing feedback on children's English language use requires particular sensitivity, especially with English learners. Preschoolers and kindergarteners are learning language, and errors are to be expected. In fact, culturally diverse youngsters may not know Standard English when they enter school, so teachers should not expect them to use it proficiently (Resnick & Snow, 2009). When children talk, adults accept their contributions with interest, enthusiasm, and praise, even when their speech contains grammatical or pronunciation errors. Feedback comes in the form of modeling correct usage or pronunciation. For example,

- S: "She goed potty." T: "Amber went potty? Okay."

Also, when children insert a word from their home language, it is recognized and accepted:

- S: "Miss Lori, look." T: "What is that?" S: "A bolsa." T: "Yes, a bolsa, a purse. Bolsa."

Providing English learners with opportunities to write offers them a chance to practice emerging skills in their new language while they are solidifying skills in their home language. Feedback on written language is given with the understanding that the way children write depends on their language abilities and fine motor skills. Writing may take a variety of forms that are expected for young learners, including drawing to represent a thought or word, dictation to an adult, or beginning attempts at independent writing. The influence of their home language may appear in writing as well. Because all of these demonstrations of emerging literacy skills are considered typical for young learners, teachers should not correct children's attempts to write. Their writing is "read" with interest and praise, encouraging children to continue expressing themselves in writing.

Review & Assessment Features

30. Assessment of student comprehension and learning of all lesson objectives (e.g., spot checking, group response) throughout the lesson

---

In preschools, assessment information is gathered through a variety of methods. Each child's progress is assessed through observations, clinical interviews (an extended dialogue in which the adult seeks to discern the child's concepts or strategies), examination of the child's work, individual assessments, and discussions with the family (NAEYC, 2009). In the kinds of activities we present throughout this book, a teacher can assess students' progress when they are actively engaged in and participating in learning activities. Children's level of understanding is more transparent when they are engaged in interesting activities than during passive learning.

Furthermore, to get the best picture of student progress, it is important to collect information over time. Preschool teachers also recognize that children learn at different rates and may develop language skills faster in one domain (e.g., speaking) than another (e.g., writing). A child make more rapid progress listening and speaking in the new language and that is fine but the teacher who keeps records over time is able to make sure progress is also being made for reading and writing, albeit at a slower rate.

In the current educational climate, assessment is a critical piece of the kindergarten program. Skill development should be assessed frequently in a variety of ways. Progress needs to monitored continuously and documented so that teachers can be responsive and flexible in the ways that students are grouped. Basing grouping decisions on data can help teachers give students the support they need to be successful. Sometimes children will be grouped with peers of similar skill level, whereas other times they should be exposed to children who are performing at higher levels. This is especially true for English learners who benefit from hearing models of English.

A word about standardized assessment in kindergarten: For many young children, standardized testing may be stressful, and the reliability of their test results is questionable. According to the Alliance for Childhood (2010), "Young children can't sit and concentrate for long. They may not understand the questions or what is expected of them. And their performance is affected by anxiety, hunger, fatigue, and stress." The authors offer a number of recommendations for parents that we have adapted to apply to teachers.

- If you see signs of anxiety that may be related to testing, be reassuring and encouraging—and consider ways to reduce test-related stress.
- Make sure parents understand that their child should get plenty of sleep and a good breakfast on testing day.
- Tell your children that tests do not measure how smart, able, or good a person is.
- If a child is overly anxious, consider discussing with parents the option to request that their kindergartner not be tested.

Concluding Thoughts

As you reflect on this chapter and how the components of the SIOP® Model apply to preschool classrooms, remember the following important points:

- Effective lesson delivery is correlated to how well the lesson or learning activity was prepared.
- Children benefit from being actively involved in meaningful, interesting learning opportunities using a variety of engaging materials.
- Feedback should be provided in a positive way that encourages children to continue experimenting with language and concept development.
- Because young learners develop language and literacy skills at different rates, it is important that assessments of their progress be ongoing.

Implementing the SIOP® Model in Preschool and Kindergarten: Sample Programs

Throughout this book we have presented ways to implement the SIOP® Model effectively with young learners. In this chapter, we showcase a number of early childhood education programs that use the SIOP® Model as a way to make teaching understandable and meaningful to young English learners. Our goal is provide you with some examples of the various ways that the SIOP® Model may be implemented in preschool and kindergarten programs. The programs we have chosen to highlight include:

- Roundy Elementary School, Columbus Junction, IA—A preschool program in a pre-K—6th grade school

- Veterans Memorial Elementary School, Central Falls, RI—A kindergarten program
- AppleTree Early Learning Public Charter School, D.C. Prep Academy, and Early Childhood Academy, Washington, DC—three charter preschools in the AppleTree Institute for Education Innovation Partnership

Roundy Elementary School, Columbus Junction, Iowa

This district has made a significant commitment to SIOP® professional development for all teachers, pre-K through grade 12. Curriculum Director and ESL Coordinator, Tara Paul, draws on her own SIOP® training to lead her district's professional development efforts. The district has one elementary school, Roundy Elementary School, which houses a pre-K program within a pre-K through 6th grade building.

In 2010–2011, Roundy Elementary School offered four pre-K classes, each with approximately 12 students. Of the 48 children served in the program, the 6 three-year-olds were identified for special education services, the 35 four-year-olds were a mix of special education and general education students, and the 7 five-year-olds were in general education. The demographic information was as follows: 81% were from low SES families, 33% qualified for special education services, 69% were Hispanic, 15% were from migrant families, and 13% were from homeless families.

The preschool teachers have been through the same SIOP® Model professional development as the K–6 teachers, and they are held to the same expectations with regard to lesson planning and implementation. Each week, teachers turn in lesson plans with content and language objectives. (Instructional time for a pre-K lesson is approximately 15–20 minutes and some lessons are presented over two days.)

The professional development program in 2009–2010 lasted for three consecutive days in the first year and provided in-depth training on three components: Lesson Preparation, Building Background, and Comprehensible Input after an overview of the eight components of the SIOP® Model. Teachers' lesson plans reflected the in-depth component trainings, and the teachers were only responsible for incorporating those three components and their features. Also, Mrs. Paul's observation of lessons focused on one component at a time. The schedule for learning and practicing each component was: Lesson Preparation—September through November; Building Background—November through March; and Comprehensible Input—March through May.

At the beginning of each year, teachers' lesson plans generally focus on school readiness content, but then follow the math and reading curriculum for pre-K students. There is not a significant difference between the pre-K structure and the K–6 structure in terms of lesson planning and delivery. Mrs. Paul comments: "We believe that this is due to the fact that SIOP® is good for all students at all levels. Our ECE students are coming to us with a very limited vocabulary, part due to not speaking the English language and part due to the high poverty of the district. The SIOP® Model allows us to really focus on giving our students a strong start in vocabulary, but also giving them access to use that vocabulary in a meaningful way."

It is a district requirement to post content and language objectives for students. In pre-K, content and language objectives are posted for children to see on a designated space on classroom white boards. The objectives are based on standards and benchmarks that are part of the pre-K curriculum. Content objectives and language objectives are easily distinguished in preschool classrooms because they are color coded for the students. Content objectives are written in red, and language objectives are written in blue. Pictures are used to show students about the language objective, such as a picture of a hand writing, lips speaking, or an ear listening. Mrs. Paul cites including objectives with lessons as the most successful aspect of SIOP® Model implementation. She says, "The students really understand that the objectives are their 'job' and what they are going to do with the activity. Every day both objectives are written, '*Today I will. . . .*' This is a consistent way to help the students learn those key words. Then after the lesson, the students post red checkmarks to show that they did their job and completed the objectives."

The district offers teachers a template to assist in developing content and language objectives (see Figure 8.1). As teachers think about objectives, they consider which verb to use that reflects Bloom's Taxonomy. For example, students will be able

FIGURE 8.1 *Columbus Community School District's Template for Developing Objectives*

Reading <u>Content</u> Objective

Teacher:		Grade Level:
Structure: SWBAT (Verb – Bloom's) (What - Content) by (Measurable Activity).		
SWBAT. . .		**Student Friendly:**
SWBAT. . .		**Student Friendly:**

Reading <u>Language</u> Objective

Structure: SW...		
Language Objective (For content objective #1):	**Student Friendly:**	**Sentence Frame** (if needed):
Language Objective (For content objective #2):	**Student Friendly:**	**Sentence Frame** (if needed):

FIGURE 8.2 *Columbus Community School District's SIOP® Lesson Plan Template*

SIOP® LESSON PLAN TEMPLATE
Lesson Objectives and Building Background

Lesson Date:	**Teacher(s):**
Lesson Topic:	

Content Objectives: **Teacher Friendly:**	**Language Objectives:** **Teacher Friendly:**
Student Friendly:	**Student Friendly:**
Key Vocabulary (to meet the objectives):	**Materials** (including supplementary and adaptive):

Building Background (Be **DESCRIPTIVE** about **HOW** you will: Link to Prior Knowledge, Bridge Background Knowledge, and Teach Key Vocabulary)

to (SWBAT) identify, solve, investigate, distinguish, select, compare, or create. Then, teachers think about the content and ask themselves: What are the students going to learn or do? This drives the content objective. Finally: How will learning be assessed? A sample content objective might be: *Students will (SW) be able to identify the initial sound "t" by selecting pictures of objects that start with a "t."* To do this, the teacher would have pictures with examples (*e.g.,* turtle *and* telephone) and nonexamples (*e.g.,* ball *and* dog). The language objective might be: *Students will (SW) name the objects that start with the letter "t."* The student-friendly version of the objectives might be: *Today I will identify "t." Today I will say the names that start with "t."*

Another scaffold for teachers' implementation of the SIOP® Model is seen in Figure 8.2. This template focuses on the Lesson Preparation and Building Background components and provides a guide for thinking about and planning for those components and features.

For the current school year (2010–2011), in August, teachers reviewed the three components learned previously and received in-depth training on the Strategies component. Among other elements, current professional development involves teachers observing lessons that demonstrate SIOP® Model components and features twice a month during in-service time and collaborating with one another around professional conversations regarding SIOP® implementation and peer observations.

This involves coaching, feedback, and reflection—collaboration that takes place a minimum of twice a month.

According to Tara Paul, who leads the professional development along with trainers from Pearson Education, "The biggest issue we have faced is differentiating the content and language objectives from each other since so much of Pre-K is oral. We really have not had any major hurdles yet with implementing the SIOP® Model at the Pre-K level, but I have a great bunch of teachers who are willing to make it work and who see the benefit of the SIOP® Model."

Veterans Memorial Elementary School, Central Falls, Rhode Island

In this ECE program, teacher Cathy Fox, an ESL teacher and a National Board Certified Teacher of Early Childhood, has used the SIOP® Model for the past two years (2008–2009, 2009–2010). In 2009-10, her class was composed of 20 kindergarteners who were all Latino English learners between the ages of five and six. In the past, Ms. Fox has had 1–2 students who had home languages such as Creole (from Cape Verde), Khmer (from Cambodia), and Mandarin, but the community population is primarily Latino.

Ms. Fox's class is a kindergarten ESL program in which the students are taught all their academic subjects. There is a full-time teaching assistant because of Ms. Fox's own physical disability. Six of the twenty students receive bilingual speech therapy, two receive services from the special education resource specialist, and four are in the process of Response to Intervention. Students have various levels of English proficiency according to the WIDA standards of English language proficiency: one student is at the entering level, having arrived from Ecuador in September; four students are beginning speakers of English; and the remaining students are all in the developing or expanding stages of English language learning. (See http://www.wida.us/standards/PerfDefs.pdf for WIDA levels of language proficiency.)

The school context is an urban setting with over 500 children, all of whom receive free lunch. The school's neighborhood is surrounded by poverty, drugs, and violence. Although many of the children come from loving intact families, others have experienced tragedy and have witnessed violence. Central Falls is the smallest and poorest city in Rhode Island, recently put into receivership by the state. Class enrollment fluctuates due to the high mobility rate in the community. Families frequently move among the Providence, Pawtucket, and Central Falls school departments, even mid-year.

Ms. Fox's classroom management is based on Responsive Classroom Theory. Each day starts with a "meeting and greeting," which sets the tone of respect and responsibility for the day. Her classroom is organized into four teams composed of heterogeneously grouped students. Classroom rules are simple and have the focus of helping students work cooperatively:

1. We are all learners.
2. We respect ourselves, our friends, and our materials.
3. If we make a mistake, we fix it.

These simple rules are reminders to maintain a positive, productive classroom climate. In addition, each of the four teams rotates for a weekly "special lunch" in the classroom with the teacher. This strengthens their sense of community, provides an opportunity for students to celebrate with their classmates, and enables Ms. Fox to learn more about her students.

Kindergarten is full day, and the literacy and math blocks are the same for kindergarten and first grade. The daily schedule consists of the following: morning meeting and greeting, reading/writing workshop (two-hour block), 50 minute specials (art, music, health, physical education or library), math (one hour-block), and science/social studies, taught thematically (45 minutes). The teacher, Ms. Fox, integrates language goals into all her instruction.

Figures 8.3, 8.4, and 8.5 show examples of lesson plans. As you can see, they are linked thematically; in addition, they reflect a strong early childhood point of view in that the reading lesson integrates some dramatic play and the math lesson involves physical movement. As Cathy Fox says, "In this time of high stakes testing, it is so important for early childhood educators to integrate developmentally appropriate practice into our lessons. I know that young children are very capable of higher level thinking skills when provided with appropriate scaffolding for their language levels and developmental levels."

In implementing the SIOP® Model, Ms. Fox said that her greatest challenge was writing objectives in "kid-friendly language" and truly integrating them into her lessons. In her case, the content objectives are dictated by the Rhode Island GLEs (grade level expectations) as well as the curriculum mandated by the school district. Her language objectives are based on the WIDA standards. She said that she finds the "Can-do" indicators particularly helpful in creating the language objectives. (See http://www.wida.us/standards/CAN_DOs.pdf for Can Do indicators.)

Ms. Fox posts lesson objectives using inexpensive clear Lucite frames that stand up. She types the objectives in a large, kid-friendly font, adding pictures, colors, or language stems to aid comprehension, and places them in the frames. She reads the objectives aloud first; then the students participate in a shared reading.

Although Ms. Fox initially found writing objectives challenging, she cites this task as the most successful aspect of the SIOP® Model for her and believes it has had the greatest positive impact on her instructional practice. She says that posting the objectives and reviewing them with the students keeps her focused and also provides the students with a purpose for learning each day.

When Ms. Fox was asked about using the SIOP® Model with young learners, she gave the following advice based on her considerable expertise in early childhood education and extensive professional development on English learners:

- I believe it is extremely important that play and active involvement be integrated into the SIOP® lesson. While the SIOP® Model features include hands-on materials and manipulatives as well as high student engagement, it is critical to maintain a balance of physical movement and quiet activities with young learners. Preschoolers and kindergarten students learn best through a variety of play experiences, which need to be skillfully planned to optimize learning. The play experiences need to be varied and include opportunities for the children to

FIGURE 8.3 *Adapted from Cathy Fox's SIOP® Reading Lesson Plan*

SIOP® LESSON PLAN: *Reading: Kindergarten*

Suggested Differentiation Strategies

Vocabulary

For lower proficiency students the teacher will be sure to include books about the "neighborhood" theme on their reading level to reinforce that vocabulary as well.

Cultural Objectives

In addition to the language & content objectives, it is key to have cultural objectives for ELs. While it is overwhelming to put these in writing for the students, embedded in my instruction is the objective that I will support the students in comparing our experience at the local Colombian restaurant to other dining experiences they have had in their native countries.

Background:
Guided reading groups for Kindergarten begin in January in my district. Students have a "browsing basket" of "just-right" books, most of which they have read before. The class is engaged in a social studies unit about the neighborhood. We have had several walking field trips, one of which was to a local Colombian restaurant. I purchased aprons at our local "Dollar Store" and brought a variety of plastic serving trays/platters from home. Students read books from their browsing baskets, with a partner, the teacher, or independently as part of their daily routine.

English Proficiency Levels: Beginning through advanced

Grade Level: K

Standards: Grade Level Expectations (GLEs)
Reading:
Students will demonstrate understanding of concepts of print during reading lessons.
Students will self-select reading materials aligned with reading ability and personal interests.

Written & Oral Communication:
Students will demonstrate command of the structures of sentences paragraphs, and text by expressing an idea using pictures and letters.
Students will listen to and respond to stories, songs, or poems.

Content Objectives

1. We will tell about a favorite book.

Language Objectives

1. The "waiter" will introduce her/himself and welcome the "customer."
2. The "customer" will listen to the waiter read the book
3. The "customer" will write a note to the "waiter."

Key Vocabulary
- waiter
- customer

Materials
- browsing baskets of "just-right" books
- aprons purchased from the Dollar Store
- plastic serving platters/trays
- pens/pencils/markers
- Post-it™ notes

Motivation
- Ask the students to "Turn and talk" and tell their buddy **why** we do our daily routines in reading (practice our word cards, read books from our browsing baskets, and choose new books to read). Allow time for several students to share. Elaborate on their responses especially reinforcing the idea that a literate community enjoys talking about books together.
- Explain that today we are going to start a "Reading Restaurant." We recently visited a Colombian restaurant in our neighborhood. Remind students that we were the "customers" and the "waiters" served us. A "Reading Restaurant" has customers and waiters as well. We will have a turn to be the customer and the waiter.
- We will then read our objectives, which are typed in a large font and placed in a clear Lucite picture frame. Sometimes pictures are added to facilitate comprehension. The teacher reads them aloud followed by a shared reading.

(continued)

FIGURE 8.3 *Adapted from Cathy Fox's SIOP® Reading Lesson Plan (continued)*

SIOP® LESSON PLAN: *Reading: Kindergarten* (continued)

Presentation

- Model the sequence for the students. Teacher assistant (or another student) and teacher will take turns being the waiter and the customer. Teacher begins by getting a browsing basket, an apron, serving tray and writing materials. The teacher assistant/TA is seated in a chair. Teacher walks to the TA/student and says: "Hi! My name is Ms. Fox. Welcome to Reading Restaurant! Would you like to hear a story about a family who is playing hide and seek?" The teacher proceeds to read the book, modeling appropriate concepts of print.

- Upon completion, the teacher says, "I'm finished! Here is your check. She passes the Post-it™ pad to the TA, who models writing a simple sentence or drawing a happy face.

- Teacher then reviews the sequence of events, recording them on a chart:

  1. Pick a book from your browsing basket.

  2. Get an apron and tray.

  3. Introduce yourself and welcome the customer.

  4. Tell the customer about your books.

  5. Read the book.

  6. Give the customer a "bill" to pay you.

Practice & Application

- Students are then partnered.

- Group rereads the chart to review the sequence and reinforce comprehension.

- Partners then start "playing reading restaurant." They take turns being the "waiter" and the "customer" while the teacher and TA observe and offer support as needed.

Review & Assessment

- Bring the whole class together to celebrate successes.

- Review content and language objectives and discuss whether we met them.

- Provide opportunities for children to share their favorite "Post-its™."

Extension

After students have had the opportunity to practice with partners, continue "Reading Restaurant" allowing them to read to other professionals and paraprofessionals within the building. We did extend the invitation for family members to visit the classroom and students read to their families as well.

Practice & Application

Initially, partners are set by the teacher according to reading levels and WIDA proficiency levels. My usual "rule of thumb" is to have no more than a two-level span within pairs (i.e., entering with developing, beginning with expanding, level B guided reader with level A or C).

Students are encouraged to use the word wall, as well as other environmental print in the classroom to help them write. Entering and beginning students can use our simple 😊 or 😟 to "pay" as well as a one word comment.

---

play with objects, learn social play, and have opportunities to engage in socio-dramatic play.

- Having social-emotional goals in early childhood programs is critical. For young learners, at times, these objectives would be the content objectives. They need to be articulated, practiced, and assessed.

- In addition, home–school connections are essential to the success of any early childhood program. I believe that all parents want the best for their children, and I work collaboratively with families to achieve it. Effective communication with families to inform and enhance support for children's learning is an integral part of daily practice. Regular parent letters, sent home in English and Spanish, provide families with information about students' learning. Experience has taught me to keep these letters simple and short. In addition to second language issues, many of the families have literacy needs as well. I recognize their desire to support their children, and I try to facilitate their involvement by

FIGURE 8.4 *Adapted from Cathy Fox's SIOP® Social Studies Lesson Plan*

SIOP® LESSON PLAN: *Social Studies: Kindergarten*

Suggested Differentiation Strategies

Vocabulary

For lower proficiency students larger neighborhood pictures are all labeled on a thematic bulletin board with many neighborhood helpers paired with buildings and English/Spanish labels.

Cultural Objectives

In addition to the language & content objectives, it is key to have cultural objectives for ELs. While it is overwhelming to put these in writing for the students, embedded in my instruction is the objective that throughout this unit, students are encouraged to share pictures/experiences of their native countries, comparing and contrasting them to our neighborhood.

Background:

Much time was spent in the beginning of the year interviewing each other and learning strengths, likes, and dislikes. In building a community where diversity is recognized and valued, we all become known as "experts" in something. Because I have some physical limitations, I also take the time to introduce students to the fact that our weaknesses or disabilities provide opportunities for others to help us. We practice learning ways to help overcome obstacles: language, disability, or socioeconomic. This is part of a thematic unit on the neighborhood. The big ideas addressed in this unit are:

● People have basic needs: food, shelter, clothing, and safety.

● Neighborhoods have places and people to help us meet these needs.

During the unit, we have taken several walking field trips in our unique "one square mile" city. Pictures of various neighborhood buildings are posted in the classroom with labels. This is one of the later lessons in the unit. "Fish bowling" is a strategy I often use to model a new activity, so the students are very familiar with it. We have also worked extensively with the cooperative group rubric included in this lesson.

English Proficiency Levels: Beginning through advanced

Grade Level: K

Standards: Grade Level Expectations (GLEs)
Students will explore examples of services (e.g., post office, police, fire, garbage collection) provided in their own community.

Content Objectives:

1. We will **classify** pictures of neighborhood buildings to tell how they help us meet our needs: food, shelter, clothing, and safety.

Language Objectives

1. We will write or say a word **to tell** how we sort the buildings.

Key Vocabulary
● sort
● classify

Materials
● samples of student work anchor papers showing sorting/classifying
● 5 Plastic storage bags (each bag is color coded) containing:
  ● worksheet with small pictures of local buildings
  ● pens/pencils/markers
  ● glue & scissors
  ● 2 sheets of 12 × 18 paper
● Cooperative group work rubric

Motivation
● Call group together on the rug. Recall our walking field trips in the neighborhood. Remind the students that in math we have been learning about different shapes and we play the secret rule game where we sort shapes into groups according to a special rule, such as "The shapes have 4 sides or they are triangles." Then we tell the "Secret Rule" about the group. Today we are going to play that game with neighborhood buildings.
● We will read our objectives, which are typed in a large font and placed in a clear Lucite picture frame. Sometimes pictures are added to facilitate comprehension. The teacher reads them aloud followed by a shared reading.

(continued)

FIGURE 8.4 *Adapted from Cathy Fox's SIOP® Social Studies Lesson Plan (continued)*

SIOP® LESSON PLAN: *Social Studies: Kindergarten* *(continued)*

Presentation

As lower proficiency students are incorporated into the "fish bowl" activity I would encourage them to use their native language if they are unable to participate in English. Students translate for each other. More advanced speakers will be encouraged to give multiple labels for the buildings.

Practice & Application

Cooperative groups will be assigned by the teacher, according to WIDA proficiency levels. I usually try to limit my cooperative groups to four students, and have multi-levels in each group.

Review & Assessment

Sharing provides great opportunities to check on social / emotional objectives. Each time I have done this lesson I am surprised at some of the secret rules and categories. For example along with the expected restaurants and markets, students have put the school and the church under the rule: They give you food.

Presentation

- Using popsicle sticks with students' names, choose 3 students to "fish bowl" with the teacher what we will do. Because many of our literacy routines use student names, most of the children can read the names of their classmates. The rest of the group stands around us, watching. To maximize student engagement, I pick a student to be in charge of popsicle sticks when I "fish bowl" and I take the role of a student. As the "fish bowl" progresses and students understand the activity, I may model unacceptable behavior, giving the students an opportunity to show their problem-solving abilities. During the modeling, I invite that student with the popsicle sticks to pick 3 more names at regular intervals give more students opportunities to participate in the "fish bowl." This also maximizes engagement. We will cut up the mini-pictures of familiar buildings from the worksheet, put them all in a pile, and take turns labeling the pictures and describing the function that the building serves in our neighborhood. Once all the pictures have been labeled, we will put the pictures facing up on the table. I will choose 2 of the pictures (i.e., Pizza Store and Burger King and model "These buildings go together because you can eat here.") I will invite the child to my left to pick another picture that goes along with mine, or find 2 more pictures that go together. The sentence starter, "These buildings go together because . . . " will be posted nearby to support students who need it. At some point I will model how to offer an alternate pair. For instance, if a student paired the car wash with the gas station, because they are both for cars, I might suggest pairing the car wash with the laundromat because they both clean things. This gives the group opportunities to problem solve and develop consensus.
- Teacher then quickly reviews the sequence of events, recording them on a chart::
  1. Work together to cut all your pictures.
  2. Name the place and tell what happens there.
  3. Pick 2 pictures if you are starting a new rule.
  4. Pick 1 picture to add to someone else's rule.
  5. Work cooperatively to glue your pictures on a paper.
  6. Write or say a word to show how the buildings are the same.
- Students go to their cooperative groups, which are organized heterogeneously according to literacy levels and language proficiency. Pass out the materials to the groups. Before students start the actual work, have them label the contents of the bag and tell what they will do with the materials. This ensures that students go to their groups ready to begin with clear expectations.

Practice & Application

- Students then break into cooperative groups, using the materials to complete the task. They are reminded that they are working in cooperative groups so it is important that everyone in the group helps with the task.
- The teacher observes as groups work cooperatively to complete the task, offering support and facilitating if needed.

Review & Assessment

- Have groups share their finished projects, allowing the opportunity for the class to guess the "secret rule." This provides another occasion for them to use their expressive language and incorporates the higher level thinking skills of analyzing and synthesizing.
- Review content and language objectives and discuss whether we met them.
- Pass out copies of the cooperative group rubric. Invite the students to evaluate their group work.

FIGURE 8.4A *Cooperative Learning Rubric*

Group Members:

_____

_____

_____

Everyone had a turn to help.					
Everyone had a turn to write.					
Everyone had a turn to talk.					
Everyone had a turn to listen.					
We solved our problems.					

= great   = OK   = not good

FIGURE 8.4B *Cathy Fox's Neighborhood Photos Worksheet*

Car Wash	Post Office	Church	School
Library	Restaurant	Market	Dental Clinic
Pizza Store	Credit Union	Health Center	Jenks Park
Fire Station	Market	Laundromat	Police Station

FIGURE 8.5 *Adapted from Cathy Fox's SIOP® Math Lesson Plan*

SIOP® LESSON PLAN: *Math Mid-Year Kindergarten*

Suggested Differentiation Strategies	

Background:
The class is engaged in a unit about shapes. At the completion of the unit, the students are expected to be able to identify and label polygons (triangles, squares, rectangles, rhombi, trapezoids, and hexagons) and classify them according to an attribute: (i.e. These shapes have 4 sides, or these shapes have curved lines.) This lesson is early in the unit. The students have already learned about squares. The triangle and its attributes are being introduced. Earlier in the day, or the day before, I will read *The Greedy Triangle* by Marilyn Burns.

English Proficiency Levels: Beginning through advanced

Grade Level: K

Standards: Grade Level Expectations (GLEs):
Students will use properties, attributes, composition, or decomposition to sort or classify polygons (triangles, squares, rectangles, rhombi, trapezoids, and hexagons) or objects by using one non-measurable or measurable attribute; and recognize, name, and build polygons and circles in the environment.

Content Objectives:
1. We will learn important things about **triangles**.
2. We will identify **differences** between **triangles** and **squares**.

Language Objectives
We will **ask** our partner to show us how many sides a triangle has.

Key Vocabulary
- triangle
- sides
- points

Materials
- assorted shapes (triangles/non-triangles)
- Chinese jump rope
- popsicle sticks, toothpicks, tongue depressors
- envelopes of squares and triangles of various sizes and colors.
- worksheet with various shapes
- glue & scissors

Motivation
- Call group together on the rug. Tell students: "Today we are going to learn about a special shape." I will hold a large triangle, asking, "Do you remember the story I read to you about the Greedy Triangle?" I will ask the students what they know about triangles, recording what they say on chart paper.
- We will read our objectives, which are typed in a large font and placed in a clear Lucite picture frame. Sometimes pictures are added to facilitate comprehension. The teacher reads them aloud followed by a shared reading.

Presentation
- I will take my large triangle and use it to show the key vocabulary modeling the **points**, and the **sides**.
- Next, I will choose 3 students telling them I am going to change their names: I will ask, "What is your name?" Student answers, "My name is Maria." I tell them, "Now you are 'Point' Maria." After I have repeated this with the other 2 students, I will tell the 3 points to move into the middle of the group and spread out. (The rest of the class will be sitting in a circle. I will take the Chinese jump rope and place it around the 3 students'

Vocabulary

Two of the key vocabulary words, *triangle* and *points* have Spanish cognates *triángulo, puntos*). I would teach these to my lower proficiency students. I would also use total physical response (TPR) when using these key vocabulary words for all my students.

Materials

All of the different shapes are labeled in my classroom on my math wall. Higher proficiency students would be encouraged to label the non-triangles by their name—rather than the attribute "non-triangle."

Presentation

During my presentation, I would continue to use TPR to support the students' mastery of key concepts and vocabulary. I would also encourage higher proficiency students to label the non-triangles, using the math word wall for support.

(continued)

FIGURE 8.5 *(continued)*

SIOP® LESSON PLAN: *Math Mid-Year Kindergarten* *(continued)*

waists to form a big triangle. I will move the rope to reinforce the key vocabulary "sides" and touch the students to reinforce "points." I will repeat the process several times making triangles of different sizes using the students' bodies as points. We will continually model the language: What is the name of this shape? It is a triangle. How many sides does it have? A triangle has 3 sides.

- I will give each child a shape. I will have 2 baskets: one labeled triangles (with illustration of the shape) and the other: not triangles. Students will each put their shape in the appropriate basket, explaining why they put it where they did. During this time I will be sure to reinforce the **key vocabulary**: triangle, points, and sides, as well as the **key content**: A triangle has 3 points and 3 sides.

Practice & Application

Practice & Application

- When we do Conga Line, I have created two groups within my class. One line would be the higher proficiency students and one line would be the lower students. This is created early in the year and established as a routine. This ensures that students get optimal interaction.

- For lower proficiency students I will have the sentence starter, "What is the name of this shape?" to support their questioning.

- I will ask the students to form a Conga Line. I will have a line of my less proficient students who will be given an envelope with assorted squares and triangles. The students will pull different shapes from the envelope and ask the question: "What is the name of this shape?" "How many sides does it have?" This will take 8 to 10 minutes.

- Children will then work with a partner to create triangles with popsicle sticks, tooth picks, and tongue depressors. They will glue the various sticks together on a large piece of construction paper to create three triangles. The children might come to consensus about how they want to use their triangle in a design or picture. For example, they want to use the triangles for a roof on a house so they draw a picture of a house around one of the triangles.

- As a final activity I will give students a worksheet to complete with their buddy, cutting and sorting shapes into groups. They will label the groups of shapes as "triangles," and "not triangles."

- The teacher observes as buddies work to complete the task, offering support, facilitating if needed, and encouraging students to use math vocabulary.

Review & Assessment

- Review content and language objectives and discuss whether we met them. Take the opportunity to reinforce the difference between a square and a triangle.

Enrichment & Extension:

Enrichment & Extension

Gross motor activities are so important for young children and the Shape Walk provides an excellent opportunity for the teacher to differentiate for all levels of language proficiency. For example, I can tell my more proficient students to only walk on quadrilaterals, while my beginners can practice walking on just the triangles and squares.

- A gross motor enrichment would be to place shapes on the floor, allowing students to take a shape walk. You could have students walk on only triangles or walk on shapes that are **not** triangles. This is a great transition activity that could be used throughout the unit to reinforce key vocabulary or concepts.

- Place attribute shapes into a bag and have the students use their sense of touch to find the triangles.

- Integrating songs and poems into the unit is extremely beneficial for ELs. Hap Palmer has some great CDs which incorporate music and movement.

- Students could go on a "shape hunt" at home, finding objects in their houses or around the school that have triangles.

keeping written communication comprehensible for the families. In addition, the home–school liaison, Mrs. Margarita Corrales, is an invaluable resource in communicating with families. She is bilingual and has strong roots in this close urban community.

- Ongoing communication with families is critical. With an English learner population over 65% and the highest poverty rate in the state, oftentimes the only way to get in touch with some families is a visit to their homes. Our liaison continues to teach me about the culture of the community and shares the hardships some families are experiencing. With her help, I conduct parent–teacher

FIGURE 8.5A *Math Objectives*

Math Objectives:
1. We will learn important things about triangles.
2. We will tell **differences** between triangles and squares.

Language Objective:
We will ask our partner the **name of the shape** and **how many sides it has**.

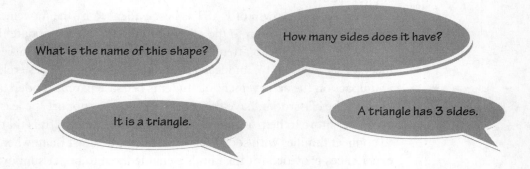

conferences on a regular basis and interviews with each family as part of a family literacy assessment. The knowledge gained from these interviews helps me to better plan for each child's educational needs. Whenever families come to visit, Mrs. Corrales is there to interpret for me. Over the years, I have learned some Spanish and although my attempts to communicate with families are always appreciated, there is still a language barrier. Flexibility is often necessary because at times, my most important communication with families happens when they arrive unannounced at the end of the day. Whenever possible, I squeeze them into my schedule because I value their input and recognize the important role they play.

• Early childhood programs have traditionally used thematic units for instruction. It is very difficult to meet the standards and fully integrate every lesson into thematic instruction. However, I strive to help my students connect all new learning with previous learning. That is why I chose to submit this group of lessons (see Figures 8.3–8.5). While the reading and social studies lessons were clearly part of the neighborhood unit, the math lesson reinforced the same metacognitive skills as the social studies lesson.

Because of Cathy Fox's commitment to home–school partnerships, seven years ago, she approached her school principal with the idea of having monthly evening gatherings for her students' families. Having worked in an urban district for many years, Ms. Fox understands that many families living in poverty are intimidated by the school bureaucracy and some have had negative school experiences. Her goal was to build relationships with the families and to help them support their children's educational journey in a new culture. She wrote and received a grant to fund Families And School Together (FAST) nights. She planned simple activities after a group dinner to include the full family. Babysitters are a luxury that many of her families do not have, so she felt that it was important that the activities include everyone in the family. The activities she selected provide experiences that engage families in literacy and problem solving. In addition, she tries to include opportunities to help families support social-emotional growth. All activities are simple to replicate at home. When necessary, materials are provided for the family to take home so they can play the game or repeat the activity. After seeing the success of FAST nights, other teachers asked to join the program. What began as an initiative for Ms. Fox's class and their families has grown to include nine classroom teachers and additional support staff.

Perhaps the growth of FAST is best evidenced by the movement of the night's meal from her classroom to the school cafeteria to accommodate the increasing number of families who attend. FAST nights provide opportunities for teachers to meet, observe, listen to, and learn from family members. These relationships have an impact on the achievement of students because parents understand what is taking place in the classroom, have the tools necessary to support the learning, and often volunteer more to help at school functions. Another benefit is that teachers are able to connect families with social service agencies to assist them when necessary. The experiences provided for the families enable them to better support their children as learners.

As you can see, the dedication of the teacher and her commitment to effective instruction for English learners has led to a high-quality program for these children.

AppleTree Institute for Education Innovation Partnership, Washington, DC

The mission of AppleTree Institute for Education Innovation ("AppleTree") is to provide accelerated early language and literacy programs to the underserved preschoolers of Washington, DC, to raise the trajectory of their future learning success. In this early childhood education partnership, AppleTree, through the DC Partnership for Early Literacy (DCPEL), works with three charter preschools in Washington, DC: AppleTree Early Learning Public Charter School, D.C. Preparatory Academy, and Early Childhood Academy. The federal Early Reading First program supports the development of early childhood centers of excellence that focus on all areas of development, but especially the early language, cognitive, and pre-reading skills that prepare children for kindergarten and continued school success. Early Reading First primarily serves children from low-income families.

DCPEL employs a full-time Language Acquisition and Family Literacy Manager (LAFL-M), Leah González, to serve approximately 575 three- to four-year-old children in the three schools. Across their partnership, half of the classrooms have English learners in them, with some schools consisting of nearly one-third EL students. Language backgrounds are mainly Spanish, Vietnamese, Arabic, and Amharic, but they also have children who speak French, Bambara, Tigrigna, Czech, Russian, Italian, Romanian, German, Tagalog, and Portuguese. The vast majority of students receive free or reduced price lunches, ranging from 70%–95% of the students at different schools. Although there are a variety of ethnicities represented, students are overwhelmingly African American in the schools. Because of DCPEL's commitment to meeting the needs of English learners and other students with low language ability, implementation of SIOP® observations was explicitly included in the original grant application.

In describing the benefit of using the SIOP® Model with young children, Mrs. González says, "All young children are learning new content and are still in the process of acquiring language skills. Many of the SIOP® components occur naturally in the early childhood environment such as hands-on activities, using a variety of ESL techniques, emphasizing key vocabulary, et cetera. However, other components, such as grouping configurations, opportunities for interaction, and written language and content objectives, and adapted content may be less common to see."

In past years, the LAFL-M observed classes that have English learners three times per year using the SIOP® protocol and provided feedback to teachers. Early Reading First grantees are required to use the early childhood-specific *Classroom Assessment Scoring System* (CLASS), and *Early Language and Literacy Classroom Observation* (ELLCO) observation tools for program evaluation, so these are used along with the SIOP® Protocol. The pertinent components of the CLASS and ELLCO observation instruments are integrated into the SIOP® Protocol to provide continuity of feedback for the teachers.

In order to use the SIOP® Protocol to observe classes with young children, AppleTree modified the SIOP® Model in a number of ways:

- Expectations for content and language objectives are different. Although teachers plan content and language objectives to guide learning, they are not required to have objectives posted. When objectives are shared with children, it is done verbally. Rules and schedules are always posted with pictures and words, and these may be objectives at times, for individual students. Selecting and writing content and language objectives tends to be challenging at first for teachers, but the process becomes easier with practice. Most of the teachers in this program identified writing objectives as an area of growth at the end of the school year. Teachers are encouraged to present one overarching objective for the children. The objective is presented orally: "We are going to practice subtraction, or taking away, in our next song, 'Five Green and Speckled Frogs'." or "In our exploration station we are learning about the homes, or habitats, of different animals. Today we will learn about swamps and the kinds of animals that live there." Throughout the day, the objectives are part of the learning activities, but are not necessarily explicitly highlighted for the children. For example, during songs, each song may represent a different objective, such as recognizing rhyming words or identifying neighborhood features. As an additional support, the LAFL-M created a document with examples of language and content objectives for teachers to use (see Figure 8.6).

- Rather than having a variety of grouping configurations as elementary school classes do, children are typically in whole group or free choice activities and only participate in groups during the small group times of the day. If a small group time was not observed, Feature #17, Grouping Configurations, might be marked n/a.

● ·

92

FIGURE 8.6 *AppleTree's Sample Content and Language Objectives*

Morning Meeting	
Content Objective	Students will identify the weather for the day.
Language Objective	Students will use target descriptive words to talk about the weather.
Storytime	
Content Objective	Students will hypothesize, or predict, what a story is about based on the title of the book and the pictures on the cover.
Language Objective	After reading the story, students will confirm correct predictions by retelling a main point of the story that supports the prediction.

- Adaptation of content (Feature #5) is less visible than it might otherwise be in an elementary classroom. The regular curriculum material is already adapted for young learners since the content itself is new for nearly all students in early childhood programs. The only time that content is clearly adapted in these lessons is when a simpler version of a story is used, or when a teacher substitutes supplemental materials from an EL curriculum or other materials they have created themselves for the regular lesson plan.

As you can see, the modifications are more in degree than in kind. The 30 SIOP® Model features are used, but are "tweaked" slightly for use with preschool children. These modifications are especially important when using the SIOP® Protocol for observations. An example of an AppleTree lesson plan on Our Community is found in Figure 8.7.

In the coming year, the AppleTree staff are modifying their program to build capacity and create additional sustainability. Rather than the LAFL-M observing classrooms with EL students three times per year using the full SIOP® Protocol, teachers will receive two SIOP® observations using the full SIOP® Protocol and be videotaped in class in the Fall and in the Spring. Additionally, they will focus on three to five SIOP® components for the year. Two components will be self-selected by the teacher and up to three will be selected by the LAFL-M, based on English learner student data. Progress toward implementing these components will be monitored during regular monthly observations.

Mrs. González believes the most successful aspect of using the SIOP® Model is that the observation and feedback focuses specifically on EL students. She said, "Teachers have appreciated the comments, especially in the feedback, with evidence from scripting to support the presence or absence of SIOP® features." The other observational tools used in the program look at the global experience of children, taking English learners into account, but not focusing on the specific interactions between teachers and EL children. SIOP® feedback gives specific ideas on how to better differentiate for the needs of pre-K English learners.

FIGURE 8.7 *AppleTree Institute's SIOP® Lesson Plan: Our Community*

SIOP® LESSON PLAN

Class Level: Pre-K
Class Periods: 5 days/ 45 minutes Lab time
Subject: Our Community

Topic:	Washington DC
Content Objective:	• We will recognize places in Washington DC • We will identify a letter of the day
Language Objectives:	• We will discuss activities in our city
Key Vocabulary:	President, monument, memorial, grocery
Materials:	cards with letters, Grocery song tape, visuals of a variety of monuments, pictures of grocery store logos (Safeway, etc.)

SIOP® Features:

Preparation	**Scaffolding**	**Grouping Options**
__ Adaptation of content	X Modeling	__ Whole class
X Links to background	X Guided practice	X Small groups
__ Links to past learning	X Independent practice	X Partners
X Strategies incorporated	X Comprehensible input	__ Independent

Integration of Processes	**Application**	**Assessment**
X Reading	X Hands-on	__ Individual
__ Writing	__ Meaningful	X Group
X Speaking	X Linked to objectives	__ Written
X Listening	X Promotes engagement	__ Oral

Building Background:	Whole class: The lesson begins with the teacher asking the Questions of the Day: What do you know about Washington, DC? Students give a few answers. T says, "This week we're going to learn about Washington, DC. Raise your hand if you know what building this is." T points to a visual of the White House. "The White House. That's right, that's where the President lives. Is the White House little, make your hands like this, or is the house big?" She continues to identify other monuments and involves children in movement to portray each, such as moving their bodies like the Washington Monument, holding arms wide like the Lincoln Memorial, making arms round like the Jefferson Memorial. The drawings of each monument are taped to the wall for future reference.
Presentation:	T moves the discussion to something familiar. She says, "While we learn about Washington, DC, we're going to learn about different places in the city. Do cities have stores where you can buy food?" Showing a store logo she asks, "Has anyone seen this sign before? This one is called Safeway. Raise your hand if your family goes to Safeway. What do they buy at Safeway? What is the beginning sound in Safeway? Sssafeway?" Children respond. T continues with 2 other store logos in the same way. Then she plays the Grocery song. Children sing along and make motions with the song. After the song, T says, "I heard lots of words that rhyme in that song. I heard the words *corn* and *horn*. They sound the same. They rhyme. Did you hear a word that rhymes with *plums*? [*thumbs*]. Plums, thumbs, they sound the same, they rhyme. What about cheese? (cheese, and please, they sound the same, they rhyme). What about more and pancake, I heard those two words. More, and pancake? [no]. "Then she points to the logos and says, "These are some grocery stores in DC."

(continued)

FIGURE 8.7 *(continued)*

Presentation *(continued)*:	T talks about other things in DC, such as the baseball team (Washington Nationals). "Raise your hand if you've ever gone to see the Nationals in Washington, DC." Then the teacher talks about other attractions in DC. "Where do you think they have pandas in Washington DC? [at the zoo]. At the zoo! So today we're going to stand up and go to the zoo. I need your help singing" [sing going to the zoo song with motions].
	Small group: In groups the teacher and paraprofessional present phonics associated with the lesson. For example, "Our letter of the day is E! E says Eh. E, E, E, E is for eggs. [sing song]. I'm going to have to take a warm fuzzy out because not all of my friends are trying their best. [read alphachant E]. Eggs starts with the letter [E]. Which animals at the zoo have eggs?
	Legs, and eggs, they sound the same, they.... [S: rhyme]. But there are other words besides eggs that start with E. Raise your hand if you know what it is. [elevator] Elevator! Let's say it together. This is an animal with a trunk and two tusks. What is it? [elephant]. When I call your name, I want you to tell me a word that starts with the letter E, and then you can go to snack."
	T draws a graphic organizer with E in the center and the words children say around it (e.g., elephant, eye, elevator, elbow).
Practice & Application:	T gives each child a card with a letter on it. She asks the children to hold the card close to their bodies without showing it to your friends.
	T: "If you have the letter A, stand up and dance, and have a seat. Please bring me your letter A and have a seat. If you have a letter M stand up and dance. If you have a lower case T, stand up and dance. Stand up on the carpet and have a seat. If you have a lower case E, stand up and dance, shake it on the carpet and have a seat. [draws each letter on the white board when it's their time to dance] If you have the letter of the day stand up and show the class."
Review & Assessment:	What are some places in Washington, DC? T points to the pictures and children identify them. T reviews each of the key words and points to a corresponding picture. Asks review question to check for understanding.

Concluding Thoughts

As you can see from these program examples, the SIOP® Model is being used successfully in Pre-K and kindergarten classes. Some issues you might want to consider in your own setting include:

- What kinds of modifications would you make in implementing the SIOP® Model?
- What level of professional development do teachers need to begin implementing the SIOP® Model well?
- What resources are available to provide professional development?
- What kind of lesson planning will teachers do to implement the SIOP® Model?

chapter 9

Effective Use of the SIOP® Protocol in Supporting Teachers

The emphasis of early childhood education is to provide an environment for young children that facilitates their cognitive, language, socio-emotional, and physical development. Teacher-directed lessons or learning activities are only a small part of the day, usually lasting 15–20 minutes each. For these instructional periods, the SIOP® Model is used as a lesson planning and instructional delivery system for teaching English learners effectively.

The SIOP® protocol, our observation instrument seen in Appendix B, has also proven useful to educators around the country since 2000, with measurable success. Initially we developed the SIOP® protocol because we found that school personnel and researchers wanted and needed an objective measure of high-quality sheltered instruction for ELs. Since the first SIOP® research project, we have interviewed over

a dozen school personnel who have told us their stories of SIOP® implementation—professional development, lesson planning, SIOP® teaching, and reflection and observation (Echevarria, Short & Vogt, 2008). From their stories and from our experience in early childhood programs, we suggest a number of uses of the SIOP® protocol in the next section. We begin with a discussion of ways that the SIOP® Model is learned and practiced so that the observation protocol can be used effectively.

Getting Started Learning and Using the SIOP® Model

In our many years of working with SIOP® implementation, we have found that there are similarities in how schools began successful SIOP® professional development. In the book, *Implementing the SIOP® Model through Effective Professional Development and Coaching* (Echevarria, Short, & Vogt, 2008) we highlight the processes that have been used effectively based on interviews with school personnel. Introduction of SIOP® components typically begins with an overview of all eight, followed by intensive focus on one or two components at a time. Most often the SIOP® components are introduced in the same order as in this book, beginning with Lesson Preparation and concluding with Review & Assessment. As you see in Chapter 8, Lesson Preparation is the foundation for SIOP® Model implementation and focus on the other components varies according to staff and student needs.

Best Practices in Using the SIOP® Protocol

The SIOP® protocol provides a tool for gauging the quality of teaching. Qualitative and quantitative information on the protocol document lesson effectiveness and shows areas that need improvement. Observation information may be used by various individuals: teachers, administrators, university faculty, and researchers. Some of the uses of the Protocol include the following:

Lesson Observation

Administrators, coaches, and supervisors observe lessons to assist teachers in improving practice. They often use the SIOP® protocol in a checklist form (see Appendix A). Written feedback is provided to teachers with information on lesson effectiveness and suggestions for areas that need improvement. This information may be used to focus on specific features of the SIOP® Model that would make teaching more understandable and effective for English learners. Researchers also use the full SIOP® protocol to measure the level of SIOP® implementation and fidelity to the SIOP® Model.

Teacher Self-Reflection

Teachers find the SIOP® protocol useful for improving their own practice through self-reflection and/or peer coaching. Some schools reported that their teachers regularly use the protocol or checklist to reflect on their own lessons, completing one after they taught a specific lesson. Perhaps even more effective is the practice of videotaping lessons and watching with various SIOP® features in mind. The objectivity a camera provides is valuable to teachers in recognizing their areas of strength as well as areas that need attention. A videotape also provides an informative view of children and ways that they are acting and interacting that may not be noticed in the hustle and bustle of the day's activities.

Professional Development

Some schools used peer coaches to assist teachers in SIOP® implementation. In one school district, a coach modeled a SIOP® lesson for a group of 3–5 teachers. Using the SIOP® protocol with the rating numbers removed, the group debriefed the lesson and discussed the components of the SIOP® Model. The focus of the debriefing and discussion was around the comments written on the protocol. Participants wrote what they saw the coach do and described it on the protocol under the corresponding feature. At the conclusion of the session, one of the teachers in the group volunteered to model a lesson during the following quarter (two-month period). Because of the non-evaluative nature of the feedback, it wasn't difficult to get teachers to volunteer. The coach assisted the teacher volunteer in planning the lesson that was later modeled for the group. Feedback from the group was always limited to positive comments and a discussion of how the lesson matched SIOP® features. After each teacher in the group had a turn in modeling a SIOP® lesson for the group, the individuals then became coaches for another small group of teachers. In this way, a large number of teachers learned and practiced using the SIOP® Model and had the opportunity to gain a deep understanding of the model.

Guidelines for Using the SIOP® Protocol in Early Childhood Settings

In using the observation protocol in settings with young learners, we offer the following guidelines:

- Provide written feedback to teachers, not lesson ratings. Although the protocol can be used for scoring lessons (each feature may be assigned a rating of 0–4), we believe that written feedback is more appropriate, given the brief duration of lessons and the nature of teaching in ECE settings.
- Focus on one component at a time. Again, preschool and kindergarten lessons are relatively short because of the children's ages and stages of cognitive development. Teachers should not feel pressure to implement all 30 features in a brief lesson. It is better to focus on implementing the features of one component well rather than giving superficial treatment to numerous features. Ask the teacher in advance which component or features should be highlighted in the observation.

- Be sure that the features are used with the needs of young learners in mind. Chapters 4–7 discuss in detail each feature and how it is used optimally with young children.

The SIOP® protocol can be an effective way of giving feedback to teachers on their lessons, providing supportive professional development. Its concrete features provide an opportunity for specifically addressing the instructional needs of English learners. The protocol is not an evaluation tool and should not be used as such.

Benefits of Using the SIOP® Model and Protocol

The most obvious benefit is that children are going to feel more comfortable and supported in a setting in which they understand the teacher, know the expectations, and have positive learning and social experiences. In addition, teachers have a concrete guide for delivering lessons that have been shown to improve the performance of English learners (Echevarria, Short & Powers, 2006; Echevarria et al., in press; Short, Fidelman & Louguit, in press). Further, it has been reported from a number of sources that school-wide use of the SIOP® Model and protocol provides a number of benefits. These include:

- A common language and conceptual framework from which to work and develop a community of practice. School site administrators commented that the features of the SIOP® Model bring together in one place many of the ideas and techniques staff have learned through college courses or through district professional development efforts. For example, a school staff may have received inservice training in cooperative learning or differentiated instruction, but teachers struggle with how to incorporate these varied ideas into their teaching practice. The SIOP® Model provides a framework for systematically addressing and incorporating a variety of techniques into one's teaching practice.

- A way for administrators and supervisors to understand high–quality instruction for English learners. Administrators and supervisors are responsible for observing and providing feedback to teaching personnel, but they typically do not have the same opportunity to learn about effective instructional practices as do the teachers on their staff. The SIOP® protocol gives administrators a means of providing clear, concrete feedback to the teachers they observe. The format of the protocol has space for writing comments that will be constructive for improving instruction for English learners.

- Information for university courses. University faculty have found the SIOP® Model and protocol to be useful in courses that specifically address the needs of young English learners. The ideal situation is a collaborative effort between teacher preparation programs and schools (preschools, child development centers, Head Start programs, and elementary schools) in which all stake holders know and use the SIOP® Model. In this way, there is a cohesive, seamless professional development process across institutions.

Using the Comments on the SIOP® Protocol

Comments can serve as a starting point for a collaborative discussion between a teacher and a supervisor or among a group of teachers. We are familiar with some ECE programs, particularly kindergarten classes, in which protocol scores are used. If lessons are rated, comments supporting the scores are essential.

The heading on the first page of the SIOP® protocol is fairly self-explanatory (see Appendix A). It is intended to provide a context for the lesson being observed. There is space for the observer's name and the date of the observation. Other information, such as the teacher's name, grade of the class being observed (pre-K or K), ESL level of the students, and the academic content area, should also be recorded. For preschool settings, instead of academic content area, the observer would note the learning activity observed. We recognize that an observation at one point in time does not always accurately represent the teacher's full lesson plan which might take several days to complete with young learners, so there is a place for the observer to indicate if the lesson is part of a multi-day unit or is a single-day lesson. For researchers and others who are using the rating scale, there is a box for the total score the teacher received on the SIOP® protocol.

A post-observation discussion with the teacher provides an effective forum for professional growth. The comments on the protocol (by component or by feature depending on the format used) offer data that can flesh out the discussion. We also get valuable information from teachers when they explain a student's behavior or clarify why something may not have taken place despite the lesson plan that included it, for example. The discussion may take place between the teacher and the observer, or a group of teachers may meet on a regular basis to provide feedback to one another and assist in refining their teaching.

As mentioned previously, we have found that it is useful to videotape lessons and analyze them later. Teachers, coaches, supervisors, and researchers alike have used this option as an effective way of recording and measuring teachers' growth over time. The tape number may be written on the protocol or checklist to indicate its corresponding lesson. Some teachers record their own lessons and watch them later. If you plan to use the protocol for rating lessons, please read Chapter 11 of *Making Content Comprehensible for Elementary English Learners: The SIOP® Model* (2010a) for a full discussion of using and scoring the SIOP® protocol with examples given. For use in early childhood settings, we recommend that written feedback be provided to teachers so that they can deepen their understanding of effective instruction for English learners and improve their practice.

Reliability and Validity of the SIOP® Protocol

As researchers, it was important to us to ensure the protocol could be used reliably (i.e., with similar results across different observers) and was valid (i.e., measured what it intended to measure). So, after several years of field-testing the SIOP® protocol, a study was conducted to establish the validity and reliability of the observation instrument. It was found to be a highly reliable and valid measure of sheltered instruction (Guarino, Echevarria, Short, Schick, Forbes, & Rueda, 2001). Experienced observers of classroom instruction (i.e., teacher education faculty who supervise student teachers) who were *not* trained in the SIOP® Model were able to use the protocol successfully to distinguish between high and low implementers of the model. A statistical analysis revealed an interrater correlation of 0.90.

Concluding Thoughts

As you reflect on this chapter and how to use the SIOP® protocol effectively, remember the following important points:

- The SIOP® protocol provides a tool for gauging the quality of teaching. It is used for teacher self-reflection, observation, and professional development.

- Written feedback about observed SIOP® features is more appropriate than using the rating scale. The brief duration of lessons and the nature of teaching in ECE settings lend themselves to qualitative feedback.

- School-wide use of the SIOP® Model and protocol provides a common language and conceptual framework from which to work and develop a community of practice. Administrators, supervisors, and coaches are able to provide concrete feedback to teachers and measure professional growth.

Lesson Preparation

___ 1. <u>Content objectives clearly defined, displayed and reviewed</u> with students

___ 2. <u>Language objectives</u> <u>clearly defined, displayed and reviewed</u> with students

___ 3. <u>Content concepts appropriate</u> for age and educational background level of students

___ 4. <u>Supplementary materials</u> used to a high degree, making the lesson clear and meaningful (computer programs, graphs, visuals)

___ 5. <u>Adaptation of content</u> (e.g., text, assignment) to all levels of student proficiency

___ 6. <u>Meaningful activities</u> that integrate lesson concepts (e.g., interviews, letter writing, simulations, models) with language practice opportunities for reading, writing, listening, and/or speaking

Building Background

___ 7. <u>Concepts explicitly linked to students' background</u> experiences

___ 8. <u>Links explicitly</u> made between <u>past learning and new concepts</u>

___ 9. <u>Key vocabulary emphasized</u> (e.g., introduced, written, repeated, and highlighted for students to see)

Comprehensible Input

___ 10. <u>Speech appropriate</u> for students' proficiency levels (e.g., slower rate, enunciation, and simple sentence structure for beginners)

___ 11. <u>Clear explanation</u> of academic tasks

___ 12. A <u>variety of techniques</u> used to make content concepts clear (e.g., modeling visuals, hands-on activities, demonstrations, gestures, body language)

Strategies

___ 13. Ample opportunities provided for students to use learning <u>strategies</u>

___ 14. <u>Scaffolding</u> techniques consistently used, assisting and supporting student understanding (e.g., think-alouds)

___ 15. A variety of <u>questions or tasks that promote higher-order thinking skills</u> (e.g., literal, analytical, and interpretive questions)

Interaction

___ 16. Frequent <u>opportunities for interaction</u> and discussion between teacher/student and among students, which encourage elaborated responses about lesson concepts

___ 17. <u>Grouping configurations support</u> language and content <u>objectives</u> of the lesson

___ 18. Sufficient <u>wait time for student responses</u> consistently provided

___ 19. Ample <u>opportunities</u> for students <u>to clarify key concepts in L1</u>

(Echevarria, Vogt, & Short, 2000; 2004; 2008; 2010a)

Practice & Application

___ **20.** Hands-on materials and/or manipulatives provided for students to practice using new content knowledge

___ **21.** Activities provided for students to apply content and language knowledge in the classroom

___ **22.** Activities integrate all language skills (i.e., reading, writing, listening, and speaking)

Lesson Delivery

___ **23.** Content objectives clearly supported by lesson delivery

___ **24.** Language objectives clearly supported by lesson delivery

___ **25.** Students engaged approximately 90–100% of the period

___ **26.** Pacing of the lesson appropriate to the students' ability level

Review & Assessment

___ **27.** Comprehensive review of key vocabulary

___ **28.** Comprehensive review of key content concepts

___ **29.** Regular feedback provided to students on their output (e.g., language, content, work)

___ **30.** Assessment of student comprehension and learning of all lesson objectives (e.g., spot checking, group response) throughout the lesson

appendix b: The Sheltered Instruction Observation Protocol (SIOP®)

Observer(s): _____ Teacher: _____

Date: _____ School: _____

Grade: _____ Class/Topic: _____

ESL Level: _____ Lesson: Multi-day   Single-day   *(circle one)*

Total Points Possible: 120 (Subtract 4 points for each NA given: _____)

Total Points Earned: _____   Percentage Score: _____

Directions: Circle the number that best reflects what you observe in a sheltered lesson. You may give a score from 0–4 (or NA on selected items). Cite under "Comments" specific examples of the behaviors observed.

LESSON PREPARATION

4	3	2	1	0
1. **Content objectives** clearly defined, displayed and reviewed with students		**Content objectives** for students implied		No clearly defined **content objectives** for students

Comments:

4	3	2	1	0
2. **Language objectives** clearly defined, displayed and reviewed with students		**Language objectives** for students implied		No clearly defined **language objectives** for students

Comments:

4	3	2	1	0
3. **Content concepts** appropriate for age and educational background level of students		**Content concepts** somewhat appropriate for age and educational background level of students		**Content concepts** inappropriate for age and educational background level of students

Comments:

4	3	2	1	0
4. **Supplementary materials** used to a high degree, making the lesson clear and meaningful (e.g., computer programs, graphs, models, visuals)		Some use of **supplementary materials**		**No use of supplementary materials**

Comments:

(Echevarria, Vogt, & Short, 2000; 2004; 2008)

4	3	2	1	0	NA

5. **Adaptation of content** (e.g., text, assignment) to all levels of student proficiency

Some **adaptation of content** to all levels of student proficiency

No significant **adaptation of content** to all levels of student proficiency

Comments:

4	3	2	1	0

6. **Meaningful activities** that integrate lesson concepts (e.g., interviews, letter writing, simulations, models) with language practice opportunities for reading, writing, listening, and/or speaking

Meaningful activities that integrate lesson concepts but provide few language practice opportunities for reading, writing, listening, and/or speaking

No **meaningful activities** that integrate lesson concepts with language practice

Comments:

BUILDING BACKGROUND

4	3	2	1	0	NA

7. **Concepts explicitly linked** to students' background experiences

Concepts loosely linked to students' background experiences

Concepts not explicitly linked to students' background experiences

Comments:

4	3	2	1	0

8. **Links explicitly made** between past learning and new concepts

Few links made between past learning and new concepts

No links made between past learning and new concepts

Comments:

4	3	2	1	0

9. **Key vocabulary** emphasized (e.g., introduced, written, repeated, and highlighted for students to see)

Key vocabulary introduced, but not emphasized

Key vocabulary not introduced or emphasized

Comments:

COMPREHENSIBLE INPUT

4	3	2	1	0

10. Speech appropriate for students' proficiency levels (e.g., slower rate, enunciation, and simple sentence structure for beginners)

Speech sometimes inappropriate for students' proficiency levels

Speech inappropriate for students' proficiency levels

Comments:

4	3	2	1	0

11. Clear explanation of academic tasks

Unclear explanation of academic tasks

No explanation of academic tasks

Comments:

4	3	2	1	0

12. A variety of techniques used to make content concepts clear (e.g., modeling, visuals, hands-on activities, demonstrations, gestures, body language)

Some **techniques** used to make content concepts clear

No **techniques** used to make concepts clear

Comments:

STRATEGIES

4	3	2	1	0

13. Ample opportunities provided for students to use **learning strategies**

Inadequate opportunities provided for students to use **learning strategies**

No opportunity provided for students to use **learning strategies**

Comments:

4	3	2	1	0

14. Scaffolding techniques consistently used, assisting and supporting student understanding (e.g., think-alouds)

Scaffolding techniques occasionally used

Scaffolding techniques not used

Comments:

4	3	2	1	0

15. A variety of **questions or tasks that promote higher-order thinking skills** (e.g., literal, analytical, and interpretive questions)

Infrequent **questions or tasks that promote higher-order thinking skills**

No **questions or tasks that promote higher-order thinking skills**

Comments:

INTERACTION

4	3	2	1	0

16. Frequent opportunities for **interaction** and discussion between teacher/student and among students, which encourage elaborated responses about lesson concepts

Interaction mostly teacher-dominated with some opportunities for students to talk about or question lesson concepts

Interaction teacher-dominated with no opportunities for students to discuss lesson concepts

Comments:

4	3	2	1	0

17. **Grouping configurations** support language and content objectives of the lesson

Grouping configurations unevenly support the language and content objectives

Grouping configurations do not support the language and content objectives

Comments:

4	3	2	1	0

18. Sufficient **wait time for student responses** consistently provided

Sufficient **wait time for student responses** occasionally provided

Sufficient **wait time for student responses** not provided

Comments:

4	3	2	1	0	NA

19. Ample opportunities for students to **clarify key concepts in L1** as needed with aide, peer, or L1 text

Some opportunities for students to **clarify key concepts in L1**

No opportunities for students to **clarify key concepts in L1**

Comments:

PRACTICE & APPLICATION

4	3	2	1	0	NA
20. **Hands-on materials and/or manipulatives** provided for students to practice using new content knowledge		Few **hands-on materials and/or manipulatives** provided for students to practice using new content knowledge		No **hands-on materials and/or manipulatives** provided for students to practice using new content knowledge	

Comments:

4	3	2	1	0	NA
21. Activities provided for students to **apply content and language knowledge** in the classroom		Activities provided for students to **apply** either **content or language knowledge** in the classroom		No activities provided for students to **apply content and language knowledge** in the classroom	

Comments:

4	3	2	1	0
22. Activities integrate all **language skills** (i.e., reading, writing, listening, and speaking)		Activities integrate some **language skills**		Activities do not integrate **language skills**

Comments:

LESSON DELIVERY

4	3	2	1	0
23. **Content objectives** clearly supported by lesson delivery		**Content objectives** somewhat supported by lesson delivery		**Content objectives** not supported by lesson delivery

Comments:

4	3	2	1	0
24. **Language objectives** clearly supported by lesson delivery		**Language objectives** somewhat supported by lesson delivery		**Language objectives** not supported by lesson delivery

Comments:

4	3	2	1	0

25. Students engaged approximately 90% to 100% of the period

Students engaged approximately 70% of the period

Students engaged less than 50% of the period

Comments:

4	3	2	1	0

26. Pacing of the lesson appropriate to students' ability levels

Pacing generally appropriate, but at times too fast or too slow

Pacing in appropriate to students' ability levels

Comments:

REVIEW & ASSESSMENT

4	3	2	1	0

27. Comprehensive **review of key vocabulary**

Uneven **review of key vocabulary**

No **review of key vocabulary**

Comments:

4	3	2	1	0

28. Comprehensive **review of key content concepts**

Uneven **review of key content concepts**

No **review of key content concepts**

Comments:

4	3	2	1	0

29. Regular **feedback** provided to students on their output (e.g., language, content, work)

Inconsistent **feedback** provided to students on their output

No **feedback** provided to students on their output

Comments:

4	3	2	1	0

30. **Assessment of student comprehension and learning** of all lesson objectives (e.g., spot checking, group response) throughout the lesson

Assessment of student comprehension and learning of some lesson objectives

No **assessment of student comprehension and learning** of lesson objectives

Comments:

The Sheltered Instruction Observation Protocol (SIOP®)

(Echevarria, Vogt, & Short, 2000; 2004; 2008)

Observer(s): _____ Teacher: _____

Date: _____ School: _____

Grade: _____ Class/Topic: _____

ESL Level: _____ Lesson: Multi-day Single-day *(circle one)*

Total Points Possible: 120 (Subtract 4 points for each NA given) _____
Total Points Earned: _____   Percentage Score: _____

Directions: Circle the number that best reflects what you observe in a sheltered lesson. You may give a score from 0–4 (or NA on selected items). Cite under "Comments" specific examples of the behaviors observed.

	Highly Evident		Somewhat Evident		Not Evident	
Lesson Preparation	4	3	2	1	0	
1. **Content objectives** clearly defined, displayed, and reviewed with students	❑	❑	❑	❑	❑	
2. **Language objectives** clearly defined, displayed, and reviewed with students	❑	❑	❑	❑	❑	
3. **Content concepts** appropriate for age and educational background level of students	❑	❑	❑	❑	❑	
4. **Supplementary materials** used to a high degree, making the lesson clear and meaningful (e.g., computer programs, graphs, models, visuals)	❑	❑	❑	❑	❑	
5. **Adaptation of content** (e.g., text, assignment) to all levels of student proficiency	❑	❑	❑	❑	❑ (NA)	❑
6. **Meaningful activities** that integrate lesson concepts (e.g., surveys, letter writing, simulations, constructing models) with language practice opportunities for reading, writing, listening, and/or speaking	❑	❑	❑	❑	❑	

Comments:

Building Background	4	3	2	1	0	NA
7. **Concepts explicitly linked** to students' background experiences	❑	❑	❑	❑	❑	❑
8. **Links explicitly made** between past learning and new concepts	❑	❑	❑	❑	❑	
9. **Key vocabulary** emphasized (e.g., introduced, written, repeated, and highlighted for students to see)	❑	❑	❑	❑	❑	

Comments:

Comprehensible Input	4	3	2	1	0
10. **Speech** appropriate for students' proficiency level (e.g., slower rate, enunciation, and simple sentence structure for beginners)	❑	❑	❑	❑	❑
11. **Clear explanation** of academic tasks	❑	❑	❑	❑	❑
12. **A variety of techniques** used to make content concepts clear (e.g., modeling, visuals, hands-on activities, demonstrations, gestures, body language)	❑	❑	❑	❑	❑

Comments:

Strategies	4	3	2	1	0
13. Ample opportunities provided for students to use **learning strategies**	❑	❑	❑	❑	❑

(Reproduction of this material is restricted to use with Echevarria, Vogt, and Short (2008), *Making Content Comprehensible for English Learners: The SIOP® Model.*)

	Highly Evident		Somewhat Evident		Not Evident	
	4	**3**	**2**	**1**	**0**	
14. **Scaffolding techniques** consistently used assisting and supporting student understanding (e.g., think-alouds)	❑	❑	❑	❑	❑	
15. A variety of **questions or tasks that promote higher-order thinking skills** (e.g., literal, analytical, and interpretive questions) *Comments:*	❑	❑	❑	❑	❑	

Interaction

	4	**3**	**2**	**1**	**0**	
16. Frequent opportunities for **interaction** and discussion between teacher/student and among students, which encourage elaborated responses about lesson concepts	❑	❑	❑	❑	❑	
17. **Grouping configurations** support language and content objectives of the lesson	❑	❑	❑	❑	❑	
18. Sufficient **wait time for student responses** consistently provided	❑	❑	❑	❑	❑	
19. Ample opportunities for students to **clarify key concepts in L1** as needed with aide, peer, or L1 text *Comments:*	❑	❑	❑	❑	❑	**NA** ❑

Practice & Application

	4	**3**	**2**	**1**	**0**	**NA**
20. **Hands-on materials and/or manipulatives** provided for students to practice using new content knowledge	❑	❑	❑	❑	❑	❑
21. Activities provided for students to **apply content and language knowledge** in the classroom	❑	❑	❑	❑	❑	**NA** ❑
22. Activities integrate all **language skills** (i.e., reading, writing, listening, and speaking) *Comments:*	❑	❑	❑	❑	❑	

Lesson Delivery

	4	**3**	**2**	**1**	**0**
23. **Content objectives** clearly supported by lesson delivery	❑	❑	❑	❑	❑
24. **Language objectives** clearly supported by lesson delivery	❑	❑	❑	❑	❑
25. **Students engaged** approximately 90% to 100% of the period	❑	❑	❑	❑	❑
26. **Pacing** of the lesson appropriate to students' ability level *Comments:*	❑	❑	❑	❑	❑

Review & Assessment

	4	**3**	**2**	**1**	**0**
27. Comprehensive **review of key vocabulary**	❑	❑	❑	❑	❑
28. Comprehensive **review of key content concepts**	❑	❑	❑	❑	❑
29. Regular **feedback** provided to students on their output (e.g., language, content, work)	❑	❑	❑	❑	❑
30. **Assessment of student comprehension and learning** of all lesson objectives (e.g., spot checking, group response) throughout the lesson *Comments:*	❑	❑	❑	❑	❑

There is a solid and growing research base that supports the efficacy of the SIOP® Model. Some of the research was conducted by the developers of the SIOP® Model through national research centers with quasi-experimental and experimental designs. Other research studies funded by philanthropic organizations and program evaluations funded by school districts have also examined the effects of the SIOP® Model on student achievement. We provide brief summaries of these studies below. We encourage you to look at www.cal.org and www.siopinstitute.net for updates and final results of ongoing research studies.

NATIONAL RESEARCH STUDIES

Center for Research on Education, Diversity & Excellence (CREDE)

The original research study that developed the SIOP® Model, "The Effects of Sheltered Instruction on the Achievement of Limited English Proficient Students," was a seven year project (1996–2003) conducted for the Center for Research on Education, Diversity & Excellence (CREDE), a national research center funded by the U.S. Department of Education, Office of Educational Research and Improvement (now known as the Institute of Education Sciences). This project worked with middle school teachers in four large metropolitan school districts—two on the East Coast and two on the West Coast—to identify key practices for making subject matter content comprehensible for English learners. Such an approach for teaching English learners is called sheltered instruction or in some regions, SDAIE (specially designed academic instruction in English). The project also set out to develop a professional development model to enable more teachers to use sheltered instruction effectively in their classrooms. Dr. Jana Echevarria of California State University, Long Beach, and Dr. Deborah Short of the Center for Applied Linguistics in Washington, DC, were co–project investigators.

Although sheltered instruction had been widely advocated as an effective instructional strategy for language minority students, when this study began there had been little agreement among practitioners as to what sheltered instruction should look like in the classroom and few research investigations measuring what constituted an effective sheltered lesson. This project therefore set the following goals: (1) develop an explicit model of sheltered instruction, (2) use that model to train teachers in effective sheltered strategies, and (3) conduct field experiments and collect data to evaluate teacher change and the effects of sheltered instruction on LEP students' English language development and content knowledge.

This research project involved the active collaboration of practicing middle school teachers, both in refining the model of sheltered instruction and in implementing it in their classrooms. In the first two years of the project, we identified, based on literature review and classroom research, effective teaching strategies involved in sheltered instruction. The model began as a research observation instrument, the Sheltered Instruction Observation Protocol (SIOP®), so that researchers could determine how well teachers were including these features of effective sheltered instruction in their lessons. Drawing from the literature on best practices, the SIOP® protocol incorporated topics such as scaffolding, learning strategies, literacy techniques, and use of meaningful curricula and materials. Our goal was to determine which combination of best practices in one instructional framework, the SIOP®, would yield positive achievement results for English learners. In addition to making the subject matter more comprehensible to ELs, we also wanted to promote their academic English growth.

With feedback from the teachers, the protocol evolved into a lesson planning and delivery approach, the SIOP® Model (Echevarria, Vogt, & Short, 2000, 2008; Short & Echevarria, 1999). It is composed of 30 items grouped into 8 components essential for making content comprehensible for English learners—Lesson Preparation, Building Background, Comprehensible Input, Strategies, Interaction, Practice & Application, Lesson Delivery, and Review & Assessment. The SIOP® Model shares many features recommended for high-quality instruction for all students, but adds key features for the academic success of students learning through a second language, such as including language objectives in every content lesson, developing background knowledge among the students, and attending to specific academic literacy skills. This model can be applied in ESL classes as well as all content area classes because it offers a framework for instruction that incorporates best practices for teaching both language and content.

After several years of field-testing the SIOP® protocol, a study was conducted to establish the validity and reliability of the observation instrument. It was found to be a highly reliable and valid measure of sheltered instruction (Guarino, Echevarria, Short, Schick, Forbes, & Rueda, 2001). Experienced observers of classroom instruction (e.g., teacher education faculty who supervise student teachers) who were *not* specifically trained in the SIOP® Model were able to use the protocol to distinguish between high and low implementers of the model. A statistical analysis revealed an interrater of correlation 0.90.

As part of the research design, student data in the form of a writing assessment based on the IMAGE (Illinois Measure of Annual Growth in English) Test were gathered and analyzed. The IMAGE was the standardized test of reading and writing used by the state of Illinois to measure annual growth of these skills in their limited English proficient students in grades 3–12. It was correlated to and a predictor of scores on the IGAP (the state standardized test of achievement) that was given to all students in Illinois, except those exempted for linguistic development reasons or learning disabilities. The IMAGE writing test provides separate scores for five features of writing: Language Production, Focus, Support/Elaboration, Organization, and Mechanics, as well as an overall score.

During the 1998–99 school year, researchers gave prompts to middle school English language learning students that required expository writing, once in the fall (pretest) and then again in the spring (posttest). Two distinct, but similar, cohorts of English learners in sheltered classes participated: students whose teachers were trained in implementing the SIOP® Model (the treatment group), and students whose teachers had no exposure to the SIOP® Model (the comparison group). The students in both groups were in grades 6–8 and represented mixed proficiency levels.

Results showed English learners in sheltered classes with teachers who had been trained in implementing the SIOP® Model to a high degree improved their writing and outperformed the students in control classes by receiving overall higher scores for the spring assessment (Echevarria, Short, & Powers, 2006). They also made greater gains from the fall to spring administrations of the test. These findings were statistically significant. The results indicated that students whose teachers implemented the SIOP® Model of sheltered instruction improved significantly in all areas of writing over students in sheltered classes whose teachers were not familiar with the SIOP® Model. These results match the findings from the 1997–98 school year when a similar administration of a writing assessment requiring narrative writing was given. Secondary analyses of the data revealed that special education students who constituted a subset of the English learners made significant improvement overall in their writing as well, with both the narrative and expository assessments.

Specifically, with the 1998–99 assessment, analysis of treatment and comparison groups' total scores (i.e., aggregated across the five subscales) found the participants whose teachers were trained in the SIOP® Model made statistically significantly better gains than the control group in writing ($F (1,312) = 10.79$; $p < 0.05$). Follow-up analyses on student performance on the various subtests of the writing assessment found that the treatment group performed at a significantly higher level in language production ($F (1,314) = 5.00$; $p < 0.05$), organization ($F (1,315) = 5.65$; $p < 0.05$), and mechanics ($F (1,315) = 4.10$; $p < 0.05$) than those in the comparison group, whose teachers had not received the study-developed training and support in delivering sheltered instruction. The treatment group did not make significant gains over the comparison group in their performance on the writing focus and elaboration subtests.

The project also developed and field tested a professional development program for the SIOP® Model that incorporated key features of effective teacher development as recommended by Darling-Hammond (1998) and Garet, Porter, Desimone, Birman, & Yoon (2001).

In this project, it has been found that through sustained, intensive interaction and coaching among staff developers and teachers—for at least one year—teachers can modify their pedagogy to promote both language and content learning among English learners. A number of professional development videos and other materials have been developed to support this program, and institutes and district trainings to prepare staff developers and teacher educators to coach others in the SIOP® Model have been held across the United States. (See www.siopinstitute.net for more details.)

Since the SIOP® Model was first published in 2000, the following uses for the observation tool and professional development program have been realized:

- Teacher lesson plan checklist and self-reflection guide
- Classroom observation tool for administrators
- Supervision tool for faculty to observe student teachers
- Research observation tool for fidelity of model implementation
- Program of professional development

SUMMARY: SELECTED FINDINGS FROM THE SIOP® CREDE RESEARCH PROJECT

- After five years of collaboration with practicing teachers, CREDE researchers developed a model of high-quality sheltered instruction, known as the SIOP® Model. This model takes into account the special language development needs of English language learners, which distinguishes it from high-quality non-sheltered teaching.

- A study conducted to establish the validity and reliability of the Sheltered Instruction Observation Protocol found that the instrument is a highly reliable and valid measure of sheltered instruction (Guarino, Echevarria, Short, Schick, Forbes, & Rueda, 2001).

- 1997–98: Researchers compared English language learning students in classes whose teachers had been trained in implementing the SIOP® Model to a high degree to a comparison group (taught by teachers not trained in the SIOP® Model) using a prompt that required narrative writing. They scored the prompt using the writing rubric of the Illinois Measure of Annual Growth in English (IMAGE) Test. The English learners in classes whose teachers had been trained in implementing the SIOP® Model to a high degree demonstrated significantly higher writing scores than the control group.

- 1998–99: Researchers compared English learners in classes whose teachers had been trained in implementing the SIOP® Model to a high degree to a comparison group (taught by teachers not trained in the SIOP® Model) using a prompt that required expository writing. They scored the prompt using the writing rubric of the Illinois Measure of Annual Growth in English (IMAGE) Test. The English learners in classes whose teachers had been trained in implementing the SIOP® Model to a high degree demonstrated significantly higher writing scores than the comparison group and made greater gains from the pretest to the posttest.

Center for Research on the Educational Achievement & Teaching of English Language Learners (CREATE)

This six-year project involved a series of studies funded by the U.S. Department of Education through the national Center for Research on the Educational Achievement & Teaching of English Language Learners (CREATE). The research was conducted by researchers at California State University, Long Beach, the Center for Applied Linguistics, University of Texas, Austin, Harvard University, and the University of Houston (2005–11). In the first 4 years, individual researchers investigated specific intervention studies in science, social studies, and language arts (see below for a discussion of the SIOP® study). In Years 5 and 6, findings from the previous studies informed a collaborative effort wherein the individual interventions were combined for a full grade-level effort across content areas and the SIOP® Model was used as the overall organizing framework for designing and delivering lessons.

The Impact of the SIOP® Model on Middle School Science and Language Learning is one of several of the studies in the CREATE project. This study used a randomized experimental design to investigate the impact of the SIOP® Model on student academic achievement in middle school science. Researchers developed science curriculum units with SIOP® lesson plans and science language assessments that focused on the acquisition of science concepts and language development among English learners.

The study was conducted in phases. Phase 1 was a pilot study designed to develop and refine science curriculum lessons that incorporate the SIOP® Model features and to field test academic science language assessments. Phase 2 involved two one-year studies. In 2006–07, 8 schools participated as treatment or control sites. Treatment teachers received SIOP® training, the SIOP® science lessons, and coaching. Findings from this study indicated that the higher the levels of SIOP® implementation by teachers, the greater the impact on students' performance (Echevarria, et al., in press). In 2008–09, 11 schools in another district participated as Treatment 1, Treatment 2, or control sites. Treatment 1 teachers received SIOP® training, SIOP® science lessons, and coaching. Treatment 2 teachers received SIOP® training and coaching. The preliminary analyses showed that there was no significant difference between Treatment 1 and Treatment 2 effects.

Phase 3 is taking place in the 2009–10 and 2010–11 school years to test a school reform intervention for English learners in one grade-level across all core content areas. Data collection and analyses for Phase 3 include teacher implementation ratings using the SIOP® protocol and student state test results in reading, science, and English language development. In addition, the researchers are collecting data from local district content tests and the project-developed science language tests. Additional findings should be available in 2012.

SIOP® RESEARCH AT THE DISTRICT LEVEL

Academic Literacy through Sheltered Instruction for Secondary English Language Learners

This quasi-experimental research study was conducted in the two districts in New Jersey. Funded by the Carnegie Corporation of New York and the Rockefeller Foundation from 2004–07, researchers from the Center for Applied Linguistics collected and analyzed data to investigate the relationship between professional development in the SIOP® Model and the academic achievement of secondary English language learners. One school district received the SIOP® Model as the professional development treatment; the other was a comparison site. Both school districts have two middle schools and one high school with similar multilingual English learner populations. More than 500 ELs were in the treatment district, with approximately 225 in the comparison site. Each district follows an ESL program design in grades 6–12 with some designated sheltered courses.

In the treatment site, math, science, social studies, language arts, ESL, and technology teachers participated in ongoing SIOP® Model training: approximately 35 teachers for 2 years (cohort 1) and an additional 25 for 1 year (cohort 2). Each cohort had 7 days for workshops spread throughout the year, and cohort 1 had 3 follow-up days in the second year. The teachers in the comparison site did not receive any SIOP® Model training. The treatment teachers also had part-time on-site coaches who primarily facilitated after-school meetings and offered guidance in lesson design and material resources. Some coaches were able to make classroom visits. Ongoing support was also provided via closed Listserv, a project dedicated Web site, and online chats.

Researchers collected teacher implementation data (two classroom observations each year, one in the fall, the other in the spring) using the SIOP® protocol at both sites. Analyses showed that the number of high implementers of the SIOP® Model increased to a greater extent in the treatment district than the comparison district. After one year of SIOP® professional development in the treatment district, 56% of cohort 1 and 74% of cohort 2 teachers implemented the model to a high degree. After two years, 71% of cohort 1 reached a high level. In contrast, only 5% of the teachers reached a high level of implementation after one year at the comparison site and only 17% after two years (Center for Applied Linguistics, 2007; Short, Fidelman & Louguit, in press). In addition, pre- and post-SIOP® lesson plans were collected at the treatment site to measure how well teachers incorporated SIOP® Model components in their preparation. The incorporation of SIOP® features in the teachers' lesson plans improved by more than 50%.

The researchers collected and analyzed results on the state's English language proficiency assessment, which at that time was the Idea Proficiency Test (IPT), for all ELs in grades 6–12 who were in ESL programs. Analyses showed that, on average, students with SIOP®-trained teachers (in the treatment district) outperformed students without SIOP®-trained teachers (in the comparison district) to a statistically significant level ($p < .05$) when comparing average mean scores on the IPT oral, writing, and total tests in the second year of the intervention (2005–06). There was no significant difference in first year. However, SIOP® students in the treatment district made greater gains in average mean scores on all IPT tests from the baseline year (2003–04) to the final year (2005–06) than the students in the comparison district did.

An examination of student performance *within* the treatment district revealed that, on average, SIOP® students outperformed non-SIOP® students to a statistically significant level ($p < .05$) in both the first and second year of the intervention, when comparing mean scores on the IPT oral, reading, writing, and total tests (Center for Applied Linguistics, 2007).

The researchers also collected and analyzed student content area achievement data in the treatment and comparison districts from New Jersey state tests in reading, math, social studies, and science for grades 6–7; reading, math, and science for grade 8; and reading and math for grade 11, although this process was complicated by the fact that New Jersey changed tests during the study. (In the second year, students in grades 6 and 7 had a new test, and were tested only in reading and math.) The analyses were further limited by the fact that the students in the treatment and comparison districts took these tests only once, and the number of student subjects was very small for each test; therefore, the results are not generalizable. The results showed a significant difference ($p < .05$) in mean scores in favor of SIOP® students in the treatment district on six state content tests: grade 6 reading, language arts, and total proficiency score for 2004–05 and grade 6 language arts, grade 7 language arts, and grade 11 mathematics in 2005–06. There was a significant difference ($p < .05$) in mean scores in favor of students in the comparison district on one state content test, grade 7 social studies in 2004–05. There were no significant differences between groups on the other 19 content tests (Center for Applied Linguistics, 2007). The content achievement results indicate some promise for the SIOP® Model, but further research and larger sample sizes are needed.

Bayless School District (MO) Program Evaluation

This case study was conducted by Pearson Education researchers at one junior high school with a student population of 41% ELs. The professional development plan was set so the building principal, instructional coach, and 9 teachers received quarterly SIOP® trainings that focused on 4 SIOP® components each year. After one year of training (and 4 components), a single group case study examined student achievement. Measures for this study were the state standardized assessments in math and communication arts. Results indicated that there was an increase in the percentage of students who attained proficient or advanced status in these areas. In Communication Arts, all students demonstrated an 8.8% increase. Specifically, LEP students made an 8% increase and students receiving free/reduced lunch showed an increase of 10.7%. In Math, all students showed minimal change; however LEP students had an 8.3% increase and students receiving free/reduced lunch had an increase of 2.5%.

Lawrence Public Schools (MA) Program Evaluation

This case study was conducted by Pearson Education researchers and involved teachers in pre-K through Grade 8 at this urban district with 24% ELs. It was a one-year "Train the Trainer" approach with a master cohort of 50 pre-K through grade 12 teachers and 15 central staff. Master teachers and Pearson trainers provided professional development for teachers district-wide with a focus on 4 components each year. Data for the study were drawn from scores on the Measures of Academic Progress (MAP) and the state standardized assessment. Results showed increases in the percentage of basic and above performance across all grade levels for MAP Reading and Math. By grade, the highest increases after one year were 19% for Reading, and 29% for Math in grade 2. On the state assessment the number of EL elementary and middle school students earning scores in the Warning category decreased by as much as 20%, while as much as a 5% increase was noted in the Proficient or Advanced categories.

references

Adger, C. T., Snow, C. E., & Christian, D. (Eds.). (2010). *What teachers need to know about language*. McHenry, IL: Delta Systems and Center for Applied Linguistics.

Allen, K. E., & Cowdery, G. E. (2009). *The exceptional child: Inclusion in early childhood education* (6th ed.). Clifton Park, NY: Thompson Delmar Learning.

Alliance for Childhood. (2010). *Tips for parents: When kindergarten testing is out of hand*. Retrieved June 1, 2010 from http://www.allianceforchildhood.org

American Speech-Language-Hearing Association. (n.d.). *How does your child hear and talk?* Retrieved from http://www.asha.org/public/speech/development/chart.htm

Antunez, B. (2002). The preparation and professional development of teachers of English language learners. Washington, DC: ERIC Clearinghouse on Teaching and Teacher Education. Retrieved from http://202.198.141.51/upload/soft/0-article/028/28045.pdf

August, D., & Shanahan, T. (Eds.). (2006). *Developing literacy in second-language learners: A report of the National Literacy Panel on Language-Minority Children and Youth*. Mahwah, NJ: Erlbaum.

Baker, C. (2000). The care and education of young bilinguals: An introduction to professionals. Clevedon, England: Multilingual Matters.

Barnett, W. S., Epstein, D. J., Friedman, A. H., Sansanelli, R. A., & Hustedt, J. T. (2009). *The State of Preschool 2009*. New Brunswick, NY: National Institute for Early Education Research, Rutgers University.

Barrera, I., & Corso, R. M. (2002). Cultural competency as skilled dialogue. *Topics in Early Childhood Special Education, 22*, 103–113.

Beck, I., & McKeown, M. (1996). Conditions of vocabulary acquisition. In R. Barr, M. L. Kamil, P. Mosenthal, & P. D. Pearson (Eds.), *Handbook of reading research* (Vol. II; pp. 789–814). Mahwah, NJ: Erlbaum.

Bernhard, J. K., & Pacini-Ketchabaw, V. (2010). The politics of language and educational practice. In O. Saracho & B. Spodek (Eds.), *Contemporary perspectives in language and cultural diversity in early childhood education* (pp. 21–42). Charlotte, NC: Information Age Publishing, Inc.

Bialystok, E., & Hakuta, K. (1994). *In other words: The science and psychology of second language acquisition*. New York, NY: Basic Books.

Bodrova, E., Leong, D., & Shore, R. (2004). Child outcome standards in Pre-K programs: What are standards; what is needed to make them work? *Preschool Policy Matters, 5,* National Institute for Early Education Research. Retrieved June 30, 2010 from http://nieer.org/resources/policybriefs/5.pdf.

California Department of Education. (2009). *Preschool English learners: Principles and practices to promote language, literacy, and learning* (2nd ed.). Sacramento, CA: California Department of Education.

Camarota, S. A. (2007). *Immigrants in the United States, 2007: A profile of America's foreign-born population*. Center for Immigration Studies. At http://www.cis.org/articles/2007/back1007.pdf

Campano, G. (2007). Honoring student stories. *Educational Leadership*, *65*(2), 48–54.

Castro, D., Peisner-Feinberg, E., Buysse, V., & Gillanders, C. (2010). Language and literacy development in Latino dual language learners: Promising instructional practices. In O. Saracho & B. Spodek (Eds.), *Contemporary perspectives in language and cultural diversity in early childhood education* (pp. 65–94). Charlotte, NC: Information Age Publishing, Inc.

Center for Applied Linguistics. (2007). *Academic literacy through sheltered instruction for secondary English language learners*. Final Report to the Carnegie Corporation of New York. Washington, DC: Center for Applied Linguistics.

Chamot, A. U. (2009). The CALLA handbook (2nd ed.) White Plains, NY: Pearson Education.

Charlesworth, R. (2004). *Understanding child development* (6th ed.). Clifton Park, NY: Delmar.

Child Development Institute. (n.d.). *Language development in children*. Retrieved from http://childdevelopmentinfo.com/development/language_development.shtml

Clair, N., & Adger, C. T. (1999). *Professional development for teachers in culturally diverse schools*. Washington, DC: Center for Applied Linguistics.

Cloud, N., Genesee, F., & Hamayan, E. (2009). *Literacy instruction for English language learners*. Portsmouth, NH: Heinemann.

Coltrane, B. (2003). *Working with young English language learners: Some considerations*. Retrieved from: http://www.cal.org/resources/digest/0301coltrane.html

Copple, C., & Bredekamp, S. (2009). *Developmentally appropriate practice in early childhood programs serving children from birth through age 8*. Washington, DC: National Association for the Education of Young Children.

Darling-Hammond, L. (1998). Teacher learning that supports student learning. *Educational Leadership, 55,* 6–11.

Echevarria, J., & Graves, A. (2010). *Sheltered content instruction: Teaching English learners with diverse abilities* (4th ed.). Boston, MA: Allyn & Bacon.

Echevarria, J., Richards-Tutor, C., Chinn, V., & Ratleff, P. (2011). Did they get it? The role of fidelity in teaching English Learners. *Journal of Adolescent and Adult Literacy*, *54*(6), 425–434.

Echevarria, J., Short, D., & Powers, K. (2006). School reform and standards-based education: An instructional model for English language learners. *Journal of Educational Research, 99*(4), 195–210.

Echevarria, J., Short, D., & Vogt, M. (2008). *Implementing the SIOP® model through effective professional development and coaching*. Boston, MA: Allyn & Bacon.

Echevarria, J., & Vogt, M. (2011). *RTI and English learners: Making it happen*. Boston, MA: Allyn & Bacon.

Echevarria, J., Vogt, M.E., & Short, D. (2000). *Making content comprehensible for English language learners: The SIOP® Model*. Boston, MA: Allyn & Bacon.

Echevarria, J., Vogt, M. E., & Short, D. (2004). *Making content comprehensible for English learners: The SIOP® Model* (2nd ed). Boston: Pearson/Allyn & Bacon.

Echevarria, J., Vogt, M.E. & Short, D. (2010a). *Making content comprehensible for elementary English learners: The SIOP® model.* Boston, MA: Allyn & Bacon.

Echevarria, J., Vogt, M.E., & Short, D. (2010b). *The SIOP® model for teaching mathematics to English learners.* Boston, MA: Allyn & Bacon.

Federal Interagency Forum on Child and Family Statistics. (2010). *America's children in brief: Key national indicators of well-being, 2010.* Retrieved from http://www.childstats.gov/americaschildren/demo.asp

Flynn, K., & Hill, J. (2005). *English language learners: A growing population.* Mid-continent Research for Education and Learning. Retrieved from http://www.mcrel.org/pdf/policybriefs/5052pi_pbenglishlanguagelearners.pdf

Fry, R., & Passel, J. S. (2009). *Latino children: A majority are U.S.-born offspring of immigrants.* Washington, DC: Pew Hispanic Center.

Fuchs, D., & Fuchs, L. S. (1998). Researchers and teachers working together to adapt instruction for diverse learners. *Learning Disabilities Research and Practice, 13,* 126–137.

Fuller, B. (2007). *Standardized childhood: The political and cultural struggle over early education.* Stanford, CA: Stanford University Press.

Gándara, P., Maxwell-Jolly, J., & Driscoll, A. (2005). *Listening to teachers of English language learners: A survey of California teachers' challenges, experiences, and professional development needs.* Santa Cruz, CA: The Center for the Future of Teaching and Learning.

Garet, M. S., Porter, A. C., Desimone, L., Birman, B. F., & Yoon, K. S. (2001). What makes professional development effective? Results from a national sample of teachers. *American Educational Research Journal, 38*(4), 915–945.

Garcia, O., Kleifgen, J. A., & Falchi, L. (2008). From English language learners to emergent bilinguals. New York, NY: Research Review, Columbia University.

Guarino, A. J., Echevarria, J., Short, D. J., Schick, J. E., Forbes, S., & Rueda, R. (2001). The Sheltered Instruction Observation Protocol: Reliability and validity assessment. *Journal of Research in Education, 11*(1), 138–140.

Hart, B., & Risley, T. (1995). *Meaningful differences in the everyday experiences of young American children.* Baltimore, MD: Brookes Publishing.

Heckman, J. J., & Masterov, D. V. (2007). *The productivity argument for investing in young children.* At http://jenni.uchicago.edu/Invest/

Helburn, S., Culkin, M., Morris, J., Mocan, N., Howes, C., Phillipsen, L., Bryant, D., … Rustici, J., (1995). *Cost, quality, and child outcomes in child care centers. Executive Summary*, University of Colorado at Denver, Denver, CO.

Heritage, M., Silva, N., & Pierce, M. (2007). Academic English: A view from the classroom. In A. L. Bailey (Ed.). *The language demands of school: Putting academic English to the test* (pp. 171–210), New Haven, CT: Yale University Press.

Jalongo, M., & Li, N. (2010). Young English language learners as listeners: Theoretical perspectives, research strands, and implications for research. In O. Saracho & B. Spodek (Eds.), *Contemporary perspectives on language and cultural diversity in early childhood education.* Charlotte, NC: Information Age Publishing, Inc.

Johnson, J. O. (2005). *Who's minding the kids: Child care arrangements: Winter 2002*. Washington, DC: U.S. Census Bureau. At http://www.census.gov/prod/2005pubs/p70-101.pdf

Kontos, S., Howes, C., Shinn, M., & Galinsky, E. (1995). *Quality in family child care and relative care*. New York, NY: Teachers College Press.

Lippman, L., Vandivere, S., Keith, J., & Atienza, A. (2008). *Child care use by low-income families: variations across states*. Washington, DC: Child Trends. Retrieved from http://www.childtrends.org/Files//Child_Trends-2008_07_02_RB_ChildCareLowIncome.pdf

Mather, M., & Foxen, P. (2010). *America's future: Latino Child Well-Being in Numbers and Trends*. National Council of La Raza. Retrieved from http://www.nclr.org/images/uploads/publications/file_AMERICA_S_FUTURE_Latino_Child_Well_Being_in_Numbers_and_Trends.pdf

National Association for the Education of Young Children. (2003). *Early childhood curriculum, assessment, and program evaluation: Building an effective, accountable system in programs for children birth through age 8*. Retrieved May 10, 2010 from http://www.naeyc.org/files/naeyc/file/positions/CAPEexpand.pdf

National Association for the Education of Young Children. (2009). *Developmentally appropriate practice in early childhood programs serving children from birth through age 8*. Retrieved July 6, 2010 from http://www.naeyc.org/files/naeyc/file/positions/PSDAP.pdf

National Association for the Education of Young Children. (2009). Where we stand on school readiness. Retrieved May 10, 2010 from http://www.naeyc.org/files/naeyc/file/positions/Readiness.pdf

National Center for Education Statistics. (2002). *The condition of education 2002*. Washington, DC: Government Printing Office.

National Center for Education Statistics. (2003-04). *Schools and staffing survey (SASS): 2003–2004*. Retrieved from http://nces.ed.gov/surveys/sass/tables/sass_2004_15.asp

National Center for Education Statistics. (2009). *The condition of education 2009* [NCES 2009–081]. Washington, DC: United States Department of Education.

National Center for Education Statistics. (2010). *The condition of education 2010* [NCES 2010–028]. Washington, DC: United States Department of Education.

National Council of La Raza. (n.d.) *Latino issues and universal preschool: Emerging Hispanic communities*. Washington, DC: Author. Retrieved from http://www.nclr.org/files/28728_file_PreschoolAccess.pdf

National Task Force on Early Childhood Education for Hispanics. (2007). *Expanding and improving early education for Hispanics*. Retrieved from www.ecehispanics.org

NICHD Early Child Care Research Network. (2000). Characteristics and quality of child care for toddlers and preschoolers. *Applied Developmental Sciences, 4*, 116–135.

No Child Left Behind Act. (2001). Public Law 107–110.

Peisner-Feinberg, E. S., Burchinal, M. R., Clifford, R. M., Culkin, M. L., Howes, C., Kagan, S. L., & Yazejian, N. (2001). The relation of preschool child care quality to children's cognitive and social developmental trajectories through second grade. *Child Development, 72*, 1534–1553.

Puente, S., & Hernandez, R. (2009). *Transforming early learning: Educational equity for young Latinos.* Chicago, IL: Latino Policy Forum. Retrieved July 6, 2010 from http://www.latinopolicyforum.org/assets/Transforming%20Early%20Learning%20FINAL.pdf

Raudenbush, S.W. (2009). The *Brown* legacy and the O'Connor challenge: Transforming schools in the images of children's potential. *Educational Researcher, 38*, 169–180.

Resnick, L., & Snow, C. (2009). *Speaking and listening for preschool through third grade.* Newark, DE: International Reading Association.

Roberts, T. A. (2008). Home storybook reading in primary or second language with preschool children: evidence of equal effectiveness for second-language vocabulary acquisition. *Reading Research Quarterly, 43*, 103–130.

Rolnick, A., & Grunewald, R. (2003). Early childhood development: Economic development with a high public return. Technical report, Federal Reserve Bank of Minneapolis, Minneapolis, MN.

Schweinhart, L. J., Montie, J., Xiang, Z., Barnett, W. S., Belfield, C. R., & Nores, M. (2005). *Lifetime effects: The HighScope Perry Preschool study through age 40.* (Monographs of the HighScope Educational Research Foundation, 14). Ypsilanti, MI: HighScope Press.

Scott-Little, C., Cassidy, D. J., Lower, J. K., & Ellen, S. J. (2010). Early learning standards and quality improvement initiatives: A systemic approach to supporting children's learning and development. In P. W. Wesley & V. Buysse (Eds.), *The quest for quality: Promising innovations for early childhood programs* (pp. 69–89). Baltimore, MD: Brookes.

Shonkoff, J. P., & Phillips, D. A. (2000). *Neurons to neighborhoods: The science of early childhood development.* Washington, DC: National Academy Press.

Short, D., Fidelman, C., & Louguit, M. (in press). Developing academic language in English language learners through the SIOP Model. *TESOL Quarterly.*

Short, D., Vogt, M.E., & Echevarria, J. (2010). *The SIOP Model for Teaching Science to English Learners.* Boston, MA: Allyn & Bacon.

Short, D., Vogt, M.E., & Echevarria, J. (2010). *The SIOP Model for Teaching History-Social Studies to English Learners.* Boston, MA: Allyn & Bacon.

Singer, A. (2004). *The rise of new immigrant gateways.* Center on Urban and Metropolitan Policy. Retrieved from http://www.casademaryland.org/storage/documents/brookingsimmiggateways.pdf

Singer, A., Hardwick, S. W., & Brettel, C. B. (2009). *Twenty-first century gateways: Immigrant incorporation in suburban America.* Washington, DC: Brookings Institution Press.

Tabors, P. O. (2008). *A guide for early childhood educators of children learning English as a second language.* Cambridge, MA: Paul H. Brookes Publishing Co.

Thomas, W. P. & Collier, V. (1997). *School effectiveness for language minority students. National Clearinghouse for Bilingual Education.* Washington, DC: National Clearinghouse for Bilingual Education.

Tobias, S. P. (2008). Slowing speech eases child's ability to listen. *The Wichita Eagle.* Retrieved August 25, 2008 from http://hosted.ap.org/dynamic/stories/K/KS_PAN_CHILD_LISTENING

Tout, K., & Maxwell, K. L. (2010). Quality rating and improvement systems: Achieving the promise for programs, parents, children, and early childhood systems. In P. W. Wesley & V. Buysse (Eds.). *The quest for quality: Promising innovations for early childhood programs* (pp. 91–111). Baltimore, MD: Brookes.

United Nations Children's Fund. (2010). *Facts for life* (4th ed.). Retrieved from http://www.factsforlifeglobal.org/resources/factsforlife-en-full.pdf

United States Census Bureau. (1990). *U.S. Census 1990*. Retrieved on June 10, 2010 from http//www.census.gov.

United States Census Bureau. (2000). *U.S. Census 2000*. Retrieved on June 10, 2010 from http//www.census.gov.

United States Census Bureau. (2005). Population profile of the United States: Dynamic version of living arrangements of children in 2005. Retrieved at http://www.census.gov/population/www/pop-profile/files/dynamic/LivArrChildren.pdf

United States Census Bureau. (2006). *Hispanics in the United States*. At http://www.census.gov/population/www/socdemo/hispanic/files/Internet_Hispanic_in_US_2006.pdf

United States Census Bureau. (2007). *Language use in the United States: 2007*. Retrieved from http://www.census.gov/prod/2010pubs/acs-12.pdf

United States Census Bureau. (2010). *School enrollment*. Retrieved from http://factfinder.census.gov/servlet/STTable?_bm=y&-geo_id=01000US&-qr_name=ACS_2008_3YR_G00_S1401&-ds_name=ACS_2008_3YR_G00_

United States Department of Education. (2010). *Title III accountability: Behind the numbers*. Retrieved from http://www2.ed.gov/rschstat/eval/title-iii/behind-numbers.pdf

Vandell, D. L., & Wolfe, B. (2000). *Child care quality: Does it matter and does it need to be improved?* University of Wisconsin-Madison, Institute for Research on Poverty, Retrieved from http://www.aspe.hhs.gov/hsp/ccquality00/ccqual.htm#quality

Vogt, M.E., Echevarria, J., & Short, D. (2010). *The SIOP Model for Teaching English-Language Arts to English Learners*. Boston, MA: Allyn & Bacon.

Vogt, M. E. (2010). *What you can do to begin developing your child's early literacy skills*. Retrievable at www.kidszonemuseum.org/blog.

Wasik, B. (2010). What teachers can do to promote preschoolers' vocabulary development: Strategies from an effective language and literacy professional development coaching model. *The Reading Teacher, 63*(8), pp. 621–633.

Worthington, E., Maude, S., Hughes-Belding, K., Luze, G., Peterson, C., Brotherson, M. J., Bruna, K., & Luchtel, M. (2010). *Serving English language learners in Head Start: Challenges, resources and strategies*. Unpublished manuscript.

index